Simple. Enormous. Love.

Or, Everything I Ever Needed to Know about God I Learned in Romans 8

By Steve McNitt, LCSW

Cover design by Olivia Wilson (OliviaWilsondesign.com)

Simple. Enormous. Love. /Steve McNitt –1st ed.

ISBN 978-1-7329149-0-2 (paperback)
ISBN 978-1-7329149-1-9 (digital)

To Susie: I love you because he first loved me. You have been so much more than my partner and best friend. I believe our best days are ahead of us!

"Let them see that this is your doing, that you yourself have done it Lord." Psalm 109:27

Table of Contents:

Simple. Enormous. Love.

Or, Everything I Ever Needed to Know about God I Learned in Romans 8

Introduction

The year was 1959. The place was San Francisco, California. My father died while my mother was pregnant with me. He was electrocuted. Not by the state, just so you know. My mother was instantly a widow who had two small children, was pregnant with me, and moved us all back to Malden, Massachusetts where she was raised and where her parents offered to have her live. I was born to a single mom, a widow in New England, a whole continent away from her friends. I was the baby of three children. Nevertheless that's not *all* of who I am; I am made up of much more than that.

When I was about two years old we moved back to the San Francisco Bay area. My mother drove herself and her three small children across country to live in California and raise them where she and my dad had started a life. Just based on the winter weather alone, I could not have been any happier. My mother remarried when I was about seven. Instantly, I went from the youngest and cutest in the family to number five, in the birth order, of six children. The sixth was my sister Laura, who was an infant that inherited the role of being the cutest. I remember, in an effort to help blend the families, I bought her a rattle. I was so excited to give her something she could play with, something that I imagined would mean the world to her as a token from her new big brother. When the moment arrived to gift her this magical noisemaker, I put it into her little infant hand. Although I had imagined her holding onto it and taking it everywhere as her new favorite toy, she instantly let go and continued back to her routine of drooling and pooping. I was super bummed out and felt like a loser; I did not realize that infants could not hold things long or yet decide which toy was the favorite. It felt like a personal blow, but then again that was never completely who I am; I am not just a brother with hurt feelings.

As our families blended, it was clear that the family structure had changed forever. The kind and compassionate words of my mother as my exclusive caregiver gave way to the not-so-kind and not-so-gentle words of my stepfather and his children. I started to doubt myself and was given ample reasons to make sure of that. I was even given a negative nickname: Elmo. Oh, not the cute cuddly guy from *Sesame Street*. It was for, as my stepdad* explained, "Dagwood's irritating neighbor kid" in the old comic strip *Blondie*. Sure, lots of kids have nicknames, but did mine have to be for some irritating neighbor? It made me feel like I was unwanted, in the way, and worthless. Although I know I can be irritating, that is not a complete picture of who I am.

When I was about nine years old I was on a Little League baseball team that decided we would all go camping for a weekend. Like so many other insecure kids, I wondered if any of the other guys (we only had guys playing Little League in those days) liked me. After all, my stepdad was President of the league, and I sometimes questioned if I was chosen for the team as a favor to him. I had never camped before and thought I was doing okay; I slept in the sleeping bag, and I did not even wet it. I did what I was told and stayed within the boundaries of the camp. A family had one of those lanterns you have to actually catch fire and keep the flame going in order to have light. When I was passing the lantern to someone I tripped. It fell out of my hand and the glass broke. Nothing caught fire and no one was hurt. I apologized, but my parents were angry with me. We did not have extra money to replace a lantern. On that same trip I sat at the bonfire one night and the smoke followed me wherever I moved. One of the other guys said that bad luck followed me. I had no idea if that were true, but they used the smoke as factual, scientific, and irrefutable proof that bad luck followed me. They started to call me "Jinx." They had me believe that bad luck was attracted to me and that it was just a matter of time before more bad luck happened to me. Of course when you hear something long enough, you believe it. I believed I was a jinx, and that if you hung around me bad luck would find us. I mean, I took that on as part of my identity for a while, yet deep down I knew there was more. I wasn't sure what, but I knew that it was not *all* of who I am.

Throughout all of elementary, middle, and high school I was busy trying to figure out who I was and listening to negative messages from others about who I was and what I would be. I used sports to figure some of it out; I was pretty good at a few sports. I used academics to figure some of it out and was able to graduate with honors, get accepted into college, get academic scholarships, and later earn a Bachelor's degree from the University of California, Riverside. Later I earned a Master's degree in Social Work. I used successes and failures to see myself, try and figure out who I was, and where I fit in the world. It was downright depressing at times, confusing most times, and often seemed like a waste of time. I think through all of those times I was still not sure who I was. Like a lot of people, I would vacillate; I let my failures define me for a while and my successes define me for a while. However, even in that mix of emotions, accomplishments, failures, and confusion, my identity was so vague and hard to define. It was crazy-making at best.

Fast forward to now: I am a father. I am an employer. I am a son. I am an employee. I am a supervisor. I am a friend. I am a spender and earner of money. I make people laugh and sometimes I make people cry. I like the movies. I love to get to speak about God's love. I am a Young Life leader, and have been for thirty years. I am married, and have been for over thirty years. I am a follower of Jesus, and have been for over forty years. Even when you add all of that up, you still do not get the complete picture of who I am.

I feel like finding out who I really am has been like a long, slow dawning of a beautifully bright sunrise while camping in the pine-filled mountains. It has been slow, gentle, and anything but radical. Over time, I have seen new places illuminated and understood them better in the mysteriously golden light as it hits them.

I think this process started when I was at Woodleaf, a Young Life camp in Northern California. I had been attending Young Life club for over a year when my goofy and loving leader, Nobie Hill, convinced me to go to camp. He swore it would be the "best week of your life." *He* didn't even know how right he was. During that week, this lower middle class misfit got to sing, have a wacky square dance, midnight swim, Jet Ski, get traumatized by a horse on a short ride, and learn about Jesus in a whole new way. I had gone to church, seen the scary and bloody Jesus hanging on the cross among the stained glass windows, that ominous music, and some funky smells. All the while people around me prayed, stood and kneeled in a rhythm I did not understand. The truth is, I only thought I knew Jesus.

I did know a part of Jesus, but I did not know him entirely. At camp, I listened to the speaker's talks, and I had some cabin time discussions that focused on who Jesus was and what he wanted. The thing that blew my mind the most was that this Jesus loved people; all people, even me. He knew about my jinxes, he knew about my family, he knew about my pain, and my insecurities. In other words, he knew me. All of me; not just the "me" I try to portray to the rest of you. He knew the actual, complete, and total me. Surprisingly, he was willing to sacrifice himself for me on the cross, love me in spite of all my flaws, and wanted to build me up in a way that would change my life for the rest of my life. I knew then that I wanted to know more about that amazing Jesus. The more I have gotten to know him, the more I have appreciated who I really am.

You see, it is only when we know the Creator that we can understand the created. I am, and always have been, created to be a Treasured Child of the Most High God. *That* is who I am. That is who I was created to be, despite any derailments that came through failures, nicknames, successes, or misunderstandings. **I am who God, my Leader and my Creator, says that I am. I am a Treasured Child of the Most High God.** The more I learn about that, the more I feel like I understand myself, my God, my roles in life, and how to make a difference in this world.

Where did I finally learn about who I am? The Bible holds a letter that the Apostle Paul wrote to the church in Rome. The eighth chapter of that letter to the Romans revealed a boat-load of life-changing stuff to me. In Romans 8 I found out about God, about myself, and about how, when we mesh together, I live a better, more purpose-filled life. Yes, I said God. He is the key to this whole thing: my life, my purpose, my role in the world, and who I really am.

God is a big deal; okay, the biggest! Thinking about him, wondering about him, trying to understand him is, well, gigantic. The complexities that surround God are mind-boggling or mind-numbing, depending on your mood. **So why is it that Jesus says it is so simple that a child should be able to understand it? I know he's right, after all he *is* Jesus.** I am so thankful he is all-knowing, because I am a simple guy; a simple guy who simply wants to understand all that I can about God. Yet, I know it is not that simple.

As I look over the landscape of our culture, there is so much information and misinformation about God. How will I know the difference? Who can I listen to? Who can I trust? When it comes to understanding God, I feel like he is *so* big and, compared to him, I am *so* small that sometimes my eyes glaze over and I am resigned to knowing that I will never fully know him or much about him. Then again, I thank the Apostle Paul for writing his letter to the Romans and explaining so much about our faith. In addition, I thank God for helping me find chapter 8, where so many incredible truths about God are sitting and just waiting to be unpacked.

I feel like the first time I actually had my eyes opened to Romans 8 is when I was a young, single, and energetic social studies teacher at Arlington High School in Riverside California, a suburb of a suburb of a suburb of Los Angeles. I coached football, wrestling, and I was in charge of student government for a minute. I was dedicated to teaching, sort of. I was dedicated to my students, totally! I coached three sports, showed them the connections and lessons that history teaches us, and I led a local Young Life club. I was plenty busy.

As every teacher knows, the secret to making more money is twofold: stay employed, and get more education. There are countless options to getting more education; many people go on and get an administrative credential and prepare themselves for professional advancement. I knew that was not for me. Many others take classes and workshops designed just for teachers. Think of the zany things a teacher would want to learn: "How to Give Your Bulletin Boards More Pizzazz" or "Using Humor in Teaching History to Middle Schoolers" or thrillers like "Maximize Your Instructional Minutes to Meet the California State Standards." So many choices, so little interest.

I knew I wanted more education, or at least the pay that came with it. I knew it would have to be something to better me as a person in order to wedge itself into my busy and purpose-filled life. I knew the one thing that never seemed to get old for me was studying God's word in the Bible. So I decided to take some classes through Fuller Seminary. I never intended to get a degree. (Not to worry all you Fuller grads: they never stooped so low, or compromised their academics enough, to have me graduate.) I knew that studying Hebrew and Greek would have been tough for me. After all, I lived in Southern California, had taken several Spanish classes, was surrounded by people who spoke Spanish, and I still could never learn it or speak it fluently. Along those same lines, I wondered if I would have to go back in time to find good Hebrew and Greek tutors. However, Fuller had so many other classes that I thought it would be enriching for me. I thought I would most likely love the content, be challenged by the environment, and the academic exercises would cause me growth and stretch me as a person.

I had *no* idea how right I would be!

Among the few classes I took was one on Paul's letter to the Romans. It was the most academically rigorous class I have ever taken in any subject. We read the whole book twice a week, taking notes on every chapter. We had to memorize sections and topics from each chapter; there are sixteen. The final examination had a series of incomplete sentences and thoughts, and we had to accurately tell which of the sixteen chapters owned that thought. We wrote papers about Paul's teaching within that book. It sounds time-consuming and tedious, at least I thought so at the time. It was not until the class was almost over that I realized the genius of my professor. He was helping us to fall in love with Paul's amazing letter to the Christ followers in Rome. How else do you fall in love with God? In order to fall in love, you have to spend a lot of time together.

When I first met my wife, Susie, I liked what I knew of her. However, the more time I spent with her, the more and more I knew about her. I went from seeing her wonderful face to memorizing every freckle and every millimeter of the scar on her chin. The more I hung around with her, the more I knew how much there was to love. The more I got to know her character and her personality, the more in depth I loved her. Although she may not be flattered by being compared to the book of Romans, our falling-in-love story was very similar. In that seminary class I spent a whole lot of time with Paul and his letter to the Romans. It is where I first fell in love with this book, which would grow into a particularly vivid love for chapter 8.

The Bible is written as a love story between people and the God who has miraculously revealed himself to all persons. It has put a special place in my heart for God's grace, which I can never repay. The book of Romans is so richly packed with grace-filled theology that inspires in us how to deal with other people, our government, our fellow believers, and our sin; not in that order.

Now, I know what the Bible says about itself: **"All Scripture is God-breathed and is useful for teaching, rebuking, correcting and training in righteousness, so that the servant of God may be thoroughly equipped for every good work" (2 Timothy 3:16, 17).** I get that some people may be offended by my premise of learning all I need to know about God from one chapter in the Bible. I know they will question my reverence for God's word. **Rest assured that I do sincerely have reverence for the *whole* Bible and I love the inclusiveness of it.** I love the flow of one story in sixty-six books. I love that different parts of the Bible have spoken to me in compelling ways throughout different phases of my life. I love that other people have passages that they hold onto, and marinate in, throughout their lives. I love, respect, and honor all of that. It's just that some people have a favorite verse, and I have a favorite chapter.

I left teaching after a few years and trained to be a psychotherapist. I have been licensed by the State of California to be a psychotherapist since 1995. In my practice I have sat with hundreds (maybe thousands, I am not that good at math) of individuals, families, and group members. I have been trained in many therapies, including Cognitive Behavioral Therapy, Dialectical Behavioral Therapy, Trauma-Focused Cognitive Behavioral Therapy, Aggression Replacement Training, Moral Reconation Therapy, and Thinking for a Change. I love the tools that I get to teach people to help enrich or rebuild their lives. **Nevertheless, I have *never* found anything that has the transformational power nearly equal to God's word.** Once you get into the Bible and the Bible gets into you, it is impossible to live a life focused primarily on yourself. We are compelled to love God and love people. As a psychotherapist, I also believe that even with the power of God's word, people need life skills to be able to live it out in our dysfunctional world, but more of that later.

However, there is no *single* place in the Bible that has provided me as much inspiration, healing, foundational faith, and hope as Romans 8. It is the one place that I know I keep coming back to for answers, reassurance, revelation, and it helps me to know who I really am in God's eyes.

So I hope that it is not sacrilegious to pick out one piece of the Scriptures to focus on. Although I must say, it feels a little like picking which is my most favorite child. (Note to Caleb and Noah: it's a tie, boys!) Conversely, I feel a little more justified when I think that Jesus only quoted from certain passages of the Bible, one at a time. Jesus announced his ministry with a passage from Isaiah 58. He did not announce it by saying "You know the whole Scripture? I came to fulfill all of that, as a whole, you know what I am talking about. You get it!" He quoted a specific part of a specific book written by a specific author.

I thank the Apostle Paul for writing his letter to the Romans and explaining so much about our faith. In addition, I thank God for leading me to find chapter 8 where so many truths about God are sitting, just waiting to be discovered. And I thank you, the reader, for coming along the journey to read my musings about this amazing slice of the Bible that has such a significant role in my spiritual growth.

Finally, over the course of my lifetime, I have learned how deep and rich the theologies of the world are. I learned that nuances of God-focused beliefs can complicate denominations, start arguments, end completely civil discussions, and confuse God-loving people. I learned that other sections of the Bible can inspire growth, encourage movements, and drive transformation. Bible scholars debate, dissect parts of God's word, and disagree over what seem like the most random parts. Yet despite all of that, Jesus said that we should not hinder someone else's faith. He also said that even a child should be able to understand it. This is especially good news for me, since I am a simple guy. I have spent the last few decades taking the potentially deep, confounding, mind-blowing Holy Scripture, and filtering it through my simple mind. This book is an honest effort to tell you about the complete makeover that we can have through The Most High God himself.

God's word has the ability to transform lives.
Romans 8 has done that for me.
I hope it will for you too.

End notes:

*I never called him "stepdad," but for the purpose of this book I will. That way you don't confuse him with my biological father, who died when I was in utero.

Before you continue out on this journey, let me tell you something else about this book. It is not meant to be guzzled quickly like icy cold bottled water after a workout on a hot day. It is meant to be sipped like a much needed and fulfilling cup of coffee on a cold and rainy winter morning when you have nowhere you have to be. To aid with that I have included questions at the end of each chapter to help you slowly digest what you are reading. May I suggest how to use them? You can answer them in a journal allowing you to write and process at the same time, measuring the impact of the chapter against your life experience. You could also read the book in parallel with a friend and then get together over coffee and discuss your thoughts, feelings, and processes; make sure you listen to theirs, too. You could gather in a small group, do the reading together, and then discuss the questions as a community. However you choose to read this book, please don't miss the opportunity to delve into who you are created to be, who God is, and how he sees you.

Okay now, let's keep it going.

Chapter 1

He Forgives When No One Else Does

"So now there is no condemnation for those who belong
to Christ Jesus. [2] And because you belong to him, the
power of the life-giving Spirit has freed you from the
power of sin that leads to death. [3] The Law of Moses was
unable to save us because of the weakness of our sinful
nature. So God did what the law could not do. He sent
his own Son in a body like the bodies we sinners have.
And in that body God declared an end to sin's control
over us by giving his Son as a sacrifice for our sins. [4] He
did this so that the just requirement of the law would be
fully satisfied for us, who no longer follow our sinful
nature but instead follow the Spirit." (Romans 8:1-4)

His name was Greg, but that's not what we called him. What we called him was just not right, no matter how you look at it. We called him "Elephant Ears." It is not my finest moment; in fact, I am ashamed of it. As a sixth-grader I was heartless, ruthless, and tactless. I am pretty sure I did not make up the name, I was not that original, but I continued it. Yes, his ears stuck out, but so do lots of kids' who are growing into their bodies. Lots of other kids had nicknames: Skinny Bones Jones and Tennis Balls, to name a few. He was called Tennis Balls because his biceps were so big they looked like someone had put tennis balls on his arms. Skinny Bones' name speaks for itself.

I had a nickname: "Chip." I was called that because both of my front teeth were chipped into an upside down *V* shape. One had been chipped when I was playing catcher in my front yard to a guy who swore his curve ball would move three feet. It didn't. The other was chipped when I was riding my bike down a steep hill in our neighborhood and a car pulled in front of me. I slammed on the brakes. To be more accurate, I slammed on the front brakes and my tooth lost a battle to the, still-undefeated, sidewalk.

Like too many sixth-grade boys, we were experts at finding people's weaknesses and rubbing salt in them. So when we saw a guy with ears that stuck out, the name Elephant Ears stuck with him. How do I know it stuck? The year was 1971, the dark ages for plastic surgery. Yet, Greg took a week off of school to have plastic surgery and pin his ears back.

Can you imagine the emotional pain that he had been in? I really don't think I can. I have thought about it so many times over the years. In most of my life I have worked with children and families in ministry, and in professional counseling. I have helped perhaps thousands of families to work through the pains that childhood seems to bring us all. And in my work I have heard firsthand the tearful stories about dealing with the damaging negative labels people put on others. In my darkest thoughts I cannot help but feel shame about treating Greg so badly that he wanted surgery to adjust the ears that God gave him. I have never really forgiven myself for that. To be honest, sometimes I wonder if Greg has forgiven me? All these years later I still feel remorse. I still kick myself and I still wish I could apologize or make amends.

I wonder if you have ever done something in your life that is so dark, so secretive, and so shameful that you have a hard time forgiving yourself? Some of us have talked so poorly about other folks that are really decent people. Some have committed crimes, big and small, that would damage our current image if we let people know. Some of us have hidden parts of our lives that we don't want anyone else to know about. Our addictions live there in those secret spots. Our pornography-viewing habits live there, how we treat irritating people live there, and what we do when we are *not* acting like Jesus all live there. Yes, God can see into all of those places. Knowing all of that, so many of us fear that God just really wants to smite us with a lightning bolt and squish us dead in our tracks. Yet the truth is that he really wants to forgive us, not condemn us; love us, not punish us.

The Apostle Paul says that even if we don't forgive ourselves, God does not condemn us. Even if Greg does not forgive me, God does. If any of us have hurt others (haven't we all?), and if those people hold onto their bitterness, God does not.

Romans 8 starts with giving us a blank slate. "There is no condemnation." This is a total pardon, total leniency; we are absolved of all of our sins and given an unconditional ruling of "not guilty" by the Judge and Jury of our eternal destiny. The only qualifier is that the pardon comes to those who are in Christ Jesus. King David wrote it this way: **"He has removed our sins as far from us as the east is from the west" (Psalm 103:12).**

This is so mind-boggling to me: God forgives my sins through Jesus Christ. How can that be? God is so beyond what I can even imagine! He forgives me. All of me. The stuff I am ashamed of, the stuff I try to hide from you, and the stuff I would never write in this book. All of it. Forgiven. No condemnation; none.

However, friends, let's not ever forget that it cost him something; something big. **"Forgiveness, which is easy for us to accept, cost that agony at Calvary. We should never take the forgiveness of sin… and then forget the enormous cost to God that made all of this ours."* - Oswald Chambers.** Our forgiveness is not free, it cost God his only son.

This is where the impact of Paul's letter to the Romans really begins to get to me. There is no condemnation if we are in Christ Jesus. His sacrifice, his pain, and his life paid the price for my sins. My forgiveness costs me nothing and costs God so much.

In case you are tempted to think that this is no big deal (or "no biggie," as the kids say) let's put ourselves in Jesus' shoes, or sandals might be more accurate. Jesus started off in heaven, the place we all long for. We think of heaven as the culmination of everything good: you can eat as much chocolate as you want and not gain a pound, you can have carbs for every meal, you can fly, you can win at ping pong, and you can finally slam-dunk a basketball even if you are only five foot ten. And in the midst of that perfect place is Jesus living his life, loving the unity with God, and the Holy Spirit. It is an eternity of love and perfection that the book of Revelation says has **"no**

more death or sorrow or crying or pain" (Revelation 21:4). *That* is where Jesus lived, all day every day.

Then again, God wanted to fix the relationship with us humans. You and I have all broken that relationship with God; we have all disappointed him, sinned against him, and needed to be reconnected, forgiven, and reconciled. He wanted to provide a way for us to perfectly (re)connect with him and to restore the broken relationships. So Jesus left paradise and came to earth. He landed in a place with no cell phones, no internet, no HD movies, no running water, and no cure for simple diseases like scurvy (whose actual cure is to eat an orange!). That is the world for which Jesus gave up heaven. He came knowing that many of us would love him, that all of us needed forgiveness, but that only a few of us would acknowledge his sacrifice and follow him. Can you image making that big of a sacrifice and then people ignoring or mocking your gift?

It reminds me of my junior prom in high school. I did not date much in high school. I only had a couple of what you would call girlfriends. Yet, I had a mad crush on a cheerleader and gymnast. Her name was Debbie. I thought the world of her; I liked her smile, had fun talking to her, and most of all I thought she was the prettiest girl in our class. When it came time to couple up for the prom, I thought I would try to get my courage up, try to pole vault my way out of the Friend Zone, and ask her to be my date for prom.

I made a plan. I knew where she was after each class, I knew the area on the grass hill where she would have the least number of friends around, and I knew where I could make my move. All of my "intel" was solid, my planning was right on. The window for success was small, but I knew I could do it. I can remember asking her in a non-flashy, try-to-play-it-cool-but-I-am-a-nervous- wreck, nerdy kid kind of way. My heart was in my throat, my palms were sweaty, I am sure my voice cracked, and I waited for her response. It was a surreal eternity and a seemingly ridiculous amount of time that lapsed. Then, drum roll please, she laughed at me. She said she thought I was kidding. It devastated me, although I tried not to show it. It was like a gut punch from Chuck Norris. She not only broke my heart, she lit it on fire, poured gasoline on it, and tried to put it out with a hatchet! I was so bummed. I was embarrassed. I was humiliated. All of that was just for asking my peer to an expensive dance.

Have you ever thought how much worse it might have felt if you were Jesus?! He came from heaven, a place so many of us long to be. A place of perfection, joy, and hopefully endless supplies of freshly baked chocolate chip cookies. Jesus walked out of perfection, took the escalator down, and landed in a grimy, tough, and somewhat inhumane time. He sacrificed so much to be a human; he endured all that the BC world had to offer in terms of disease, tough labor, and oppressively callous Roman rule.

Through his grace and forgiveness he asks all of us to the greatest dance ever imagined. Yet so many of us laugh at him, say no, mock him openly, use his name as a curse word, or deny the sincerity of his teaching and his life. He knew those things would happen, and still chose to put himself out there for us in hopes that you might say yes to a restored relationship with him.

Despite your past or the hidden knowledge and secrets that rattle around in your brain, in Jesus there is no condemnation. I have heard it said that if you were the *only* person on earth, Jesus still would have died for you so that *you* could have no condemnation, just grace and forgiveness.

I am not a religious scholar or theologian, so there are parts of other religions that I don't understand, but this seems to be the thing that separates following Christ from following all other religions. I am a simple guy who has simply tried to honestly study and interact with people from other faiths, and I think this one point is the tipping point between all other religions and what I have learned about God.

Simply put, all other religions are about people trying to elevate themselves to get as close to God as possible. We try to be good, do well, transform our minds to think good thoughts, in the hopes that we will tip the scales of judgment in our favor and God will deem us worthy. We do all of this in hopes that we will get into whatever godly next-world thing is in store for good people: heaven, paradise, evolving into a better spirit, or whatever the positive afterlife looks like for different belief systems.

In Romans 8, and throughout the New Testament, we learn that it was God who lowered himself in the person of Jesus Christ so that we could have a teacher, a guide, and a perfect example of how to live. However, what is most important of all of that is that **"there is no condemnation for those who belong to Christ Jesus" (Romans 8:2).** All other religions tell us how good it is to try and reach up to God, to get as close to him as you can. I truly believe that we are better off when we try to live better, more pure lives. But then again, I don't think that doing good works will ultimately sway the Almighty God that we have offended by those sins. Our sins are forgiven through the work of Jesus Christ when he took them on himself on the cross and died for our sins, carrying our guilt with him. **When he resurrected from the grave he showed, again, that he is our Savior, our forgiver, and the only reason that there is NO condemnation by our Heavenly Father.**

Although I need to learn it again and again throughout my life, in Romans 8 I learn that through Jesus, God does not condemn me for my sins. Even if I condemn myself, I am alone in that. God forgives. Even if those that I have hurt do not forgive me, God does. A God like that is full of grace, patience, and does not have a petty, immature, or spiteful bone is his mysterious, heavenly, body!

So what does it mean to be forgiven? What does it mean to have no condemnation from God? It means I have a clean slate. He does not hold my past against me. He knows the terrible things I have done and tried to hide. He knows, but he does not hold it against me.

He does not condemn me. What does that mean? I don't want to be too overdramatic, but when I think of someone being condemned, it is horrible. To be condemned is to be sent to a prison, locked away forever, and they throw away the key. You are dead to society, you are gone, forgotten, and people are glad to be rid of you. They do that for as many years as it takes. You will die alone and get a pauper's funeral.

The opposite of condemned is so much better. I took some antonyms and added thoughts to each one that I hope will give you peace, hope, and joy. I will **bold** the antonyms so you can have a glimpse of how God sees us.

We are **approved** by God, the Most High. We are given a **compliment** by him who calls us by name. He **lauds** our existence. He **praises** us the way a loving and perfect father would. He **builds up** our character and hopes we will feel his love at the deepest, most secure, and core level. He **commends** us for our gifts and our loving gestures. He **absolves** our sins as only he can, setting us free from our past and guilt. He **endorses** our lives in a way that it is like we have the perfect heavenly sponsor for our future. We are **acquitted** of all negative charges, **cleared** of the accusations, **pardoned, released** back into the streets, and **set free** to be the people God has created us to be. From there we get a chance to experience repentance, expressing our sorrow for our sins, and be drawn to the loving and compelling nature of God. When we do, we are sent to a heart and soul rehab center where we get a lifetime to learn and change and become ever closer to being the grace-filled person God intended us to be. We get to drink from the fountain of genuine forgiveness, joy, and goodness that God has for us. Then we get to be all of that for other people too. **We, too, learn to forgive and not condemn; we learn to change from the inside out and bring joy, light, hope, and peace to those around us.** There are so many more things included in our experience, but we will delve into those things within the chapters that follow.

Knowing all of this, I thank God for his forgiving nature. The more I believe, deep in my inner thoughts and primary emotions, that I am forgiven, the more grateful I, and others, have become. **Oswald Chambers says: *"The thing that awakens the deepest fountain of gratitude in a human is that God has forgiven his sin."** Whenever I feel like I am becoming ungrateful for what life is dishing my way, I try to remember that God has looked at my putrid sin and arranged the forgiving compassion that he has promised. He has seen me at my worst; my most shameful, illegal, immoral, and even in my most horrendous thoughts, yet he forgives me.

Sure, I have been through some tough seasons. I have been through infertility, divorced parents, death of a sibling, and have a son who has had leukemia twice. When I was going through them I did what we all tend to do: I yelled, I cussed, I cursed God's name, I feared to the bones on too many days, and I wondered why he was allowing this crappy stuff to be happening in my life. Through those times my anxiety went off the charts, my tears went off my cheeks, and I wondered if my faith would go off the rails. I call all of that normal. But do you know what is better than normal? Remembering that the God of all creation has loved me, forgiven me, and wants the very, very best for me. Remembering that is not too normal, but it is liberating, empowering, and very, very true. There is no condemnation for those who are in Christ Jesus, and for that I am so thankful. There is, however, abundant love, *and* much more to learn.

What I have learned about God so far:

1. He forgives me, he does not condemn me.

Questions to ask yourself and maybe a trusted friend over coffee:

- Why do you think Jesus left heaven to come to earth?
- Is there anyone in your life that you would give up a lot for? Who is it? What would you be willing to give up for them?
- What are some things that you need to be forgiven for?
- If God forgives you, why don't you forgive yourself?
- God is willing to forgive that person who hurt you. What stops you from trying to forgive them too?

ENDNOTES:

*Oswald Chambers, My Utmost for His Highest 1992

Chapter 2

Great Cause, Great Leader

"Those who are dominated by the sinful nature think about sinful things, but those who are controlled by the Holy Spirit think about things that please the Spirit. [6] So letting your sinful nature control your mind leads to death. But letting the Spirit control your mind leads to life and peace. [7] For the sinful nature is always hostile to God. It never did obey God's laws, and it never will.
[8] That's why those who are still under the control of their sinful nature can never please God." (Romans 8:5-8)

In December of 1997 there was a movie released called **As Good as It Gets*. Jack Nicholson won the Academy Award for his role as a quirky, neurotic, and rude author. The official movie trailer described him as an "appalling individual." He is rude to everyone, has obsessive compulsive disorder, and is generally hard to be around. His rudeness stems from him constantly thinking about himself, his needs, and how others are affecting him. He frequents a diner, where a certain waitress, played by

Helen Hunt, who also won an Oscar for her role, is able to tolerate him, give him grace, and work past her frustrations and his irritating qualities. Near the end of the movie, he has gotten so far under her skin that she may call it quits on the awkward relationship. Then she turns to him and asks him to give her a compliment "and mean it." He stumbles through a story and then says to her: "You make me want to be a better man."

That is what Jesus does for me; he makes me want to be a better man. It is why I want him to be the leader of my life. In the last chapter we learned that there is no condemnation for those who follow Christ. It is his love, compassion, and forgiveness that makes me want to be a better person. He has called me to be a better person, but he does not shackle me up and force me into some wacky slavery of goodness. He keeps my free will fully intact. I have to choose it. I know I will never be Jesus, but I can be more *like* him.

I really do wish I could be more like Jesus, but I feel like no matter how hard I try to be like him, I fall short, I sin. I make mistakes, and often my mistakes hurt myself, my relationships, or others. It is so irritating to try so hard and come up short so often. Paul knew it too. In this same letter to the Romans, Paul writes near the end of chapter seven that he shares a similar struggle. **"The trouble is with me, for I am all too human, a slave to sin. [15] I don't really understand myself, for I want to do what is right, but I don't do it. Instead, I do what I hate. [18] ...I want to do what is right, but I can't. [19] I want to do what is good, but I don't. I don't want to do what is wrong, but I do it anyway" (Romans 7:14, 15, 18, 19).** I don't know if you can relate to that, but I can. I *want* to be a better man by trying to do what is right, but then I mess it up. I don't *want* to do what is wrong, but I do it anyway. My actions and my thoughts are led by my own desires, and it does not always end up well for me or others. We hear from advertisers, and sometimes friends, to just do what feels right, but too often what feels right may not actually *be* right. It is all so confusing. The thoughts and forces that are leading me are sometimes leading me astray.

Here's some good news: If you find yourself confused by your own behaviors, you may be totally normal. Here's some bad news: unless we get better leadership to follow, we will continue to struggle with all of our same old issues. We have gotten ourselves into this spot where we sin, we mess up, and we need a Savior. Graciously, God has provided Jesus' death and resurrection to pay the price for our sins. Thankfully we can escape that condemnation. All of that is taken care of by God.

However, if we are going to be better people, we need someone who will lead us and teach us how to be the people we were designed to be. If we could have figured it out and done it on our own, we would have done it by now. That is why I choose to follow the amazing example of Jesus Christ. His life is dominated by loving gestures to others, by Godly adventures that help others, by decisions that did not compromise his relationship with God, and by wisdom that helped others to be better people. That is why I make him the leader of my life.

Yet, if we could just change, we would. **It seems like being a better person is more than just *not* doing dumb or sinful stuff anymore.** We have to have something to replace it with that will build us up, builds up others around us, and builds up our goodness muscles, so that it becomes second nature. In other words, we have to have new leadership, new goals, and a new game plan.

Let me give you a goofy example, but you have to play along. I am asking you to really engage in this exercise; don't just passively read this next section. I want to show why it is so important to change leaders in order to change thoughts or behaviors.

Are you with me? Here we go:

For the next minute or two, I don't want you to think about elephants. Don't think about how tall they are (between eight and eleven feet). Don't think about their big, floppy ears that seem so thin and sometimes look like they have been torn. Don't think about their immense, thick legs that seem as round and strong as palm trees. Don't think about their trunks, and how they can pick up peanuts and put them in their mouths, or can be used like straws to drink from a river. Don't think about their tails, which can be about four feet long, with a tuft of wiry hair at the end of them. Whatever you do, don't think about elephants.

Now then, how did you do? Were you able to delete elephants from your conscious mind? Most people, despite the plea to not think about elephants, *only* think about those wonderful animals. The same thing happens when we try to stop our ungodly behaviors. The more we try to stop, often times the more we think about it, and sometimes obsess until we meet that need. I have been on several diets where I am told what *not* to eat, and often those are the things I miss the most, think about the most, and obsess about the most.

Let's try the same exercise again, but this time let's change focus; we will have a new thought to engage in. I don't want you to think about elephants. Instead I want you to think about puppies. Imagine that near your lap right now is a furry brown puppy who is napping with her tiny head near you. Think about how soft her fur is. Think about when the puppy was awake, how tough she thought she was, and when she barked it was so high-pitched that it was endearing and loveable. Think about how razor-sharp those teeth were you when you were playing together and she was trying to get the ball out of your hand. Think about what you would name her.

How did you do this time? Did you think about elephants? It seems so much easier for me to do what I want to do when I have something different on which to focus. It is the same with my thoughts and behaviors throughout my day and my life. Left on my own I, like Paul, do things I don't want to do. I often disappoint God and sin. It seems clear to me that I need something else to lead me toward doing right, not just keep me from doing wrong.

In the middle of this important section of Romans 8, Paul places this amazing wisdom: **"So letting your sinful nature control your mind leads to death. But letting the Spirit control your mind leads to life and peace" (Romans 8:6).** Most of us have let our sinful nature control us from time to time. Paul says it leads to death:

spiritual death, physical death, death of hopes or relationships, and sometimes the death of our positive life-giving spirit. The most excellent news is that we are not stuck in that. We can let the Holy Spirit control our minds; we can have a new leader. This leader will *only* lead us to life and peace.

In the last chapter we talked about being freed from our sin and condemnation by Jesus, but needing some rehabilitation in order to change our ways. We can become better people under the leadership of God's life-giving Spirit. Then again, we have to acknowledge that we have competing desires. We have to acknowledge that we have to know how to let the right, good, and loving desires win out in the end. In other words, we will have to make choices.

It reminds me of an old Native American story that I have read on a few occasions. It illustrates what Paul talks about when he reminds us to be careful of what kind of leadership we follow, what thoughts we give into, and what we let our minds dwell on.

> **A group of children gathered around a wise grandfather and he told them this story:
> "We all have two wolves inside us, you see. They are in our chests. And these wolves are constantly

> fighting each other." The eyes of the children have grown big by now. "In *our* chests too, Grandfather?" asks another child. "And in *your* chest too?" asks a third one. He nods. "Yes, in my chest too." He surely has their attention now. Grandfather continues. "There is a white wolf and a black wolf. The black wolf is filled with fear, anger, envy, jealousy, greed, and arrogance. The white wolf is filled with peace, love, hope, courage, humility, compassion, and faith. They battle constantly." Then he stops. It's the child that asked the initial question that can't handle the tension anymore. "But Grandfather, which wolf wins?" The old Cherokee simply replies, "The one that we feed."

We all fight an internal battle. God gives us tools, lessons, examples, and his Holy Spirit, but it is you and I that have to fight the battle. God will not overthrow our free will with force and elbow us out of the equation; he wants us to love him, wants us to battle our will, and give it over to him. On the other hand, he wants us to fight voluntarily. There is no draft that gets us into these battles against our will. So we have to hope, pray, work, and strategize to make sure the Holy Spirit will win the battles in our minds. How will we know? How will we make sure? Which side wins our thoughts and minds? Like the wolves, it is the one we feed the most. So we can feed our minds and our spirit in Godly ways or in sinful ways. **In other words, following Jesus is not a spectator sport.** Following Jesus is an action verb and active lifestyle. It takes activity, thoughts, strategy, and a willingness to do things differently, just as Jesus did.

We can feed our minds and our spirits in lots of ways; in fact, we already do. However, whatever you feed it the most will do the most good or the most damage. We know this from everything we are taught about nutrition. Endurance athletes have a saying: "junk in, junk out." If you feed your body a steady diet of junk food and sugar, it will perform below par. If you feed your body only lean proteins and greens, your body will perform up to its highest potential.

Our spiritual lives are no different. If we feed our spirits a steady diet of Bible reading, prayer, good teaching, and honest and robust fellowship, we will learn and grow; we will be feeding the God-honoring Wolf. We will be allowing a new leader to lead our lives, our thoughts, and our actions. If we rarely consume worship, praise, contemplation, prayer, and God's word, why would we ever expect the God-honoring Wolf to win battles? That is a recipe for the Black Wolf to move in and have his way with us, our souls, our hearts, and our lives. Thankfully, God has given us his Holy Spirit to lead us, to guide us, and to equip us to do the right things. Letting the Spirit control our minds leads to life and peace. I seem to need more of both of those, don't you?

God's forgiveness of me, his grace, and his loving example make me want to be a better person. However, that desire alone does not make me a better person, I have to learn how. Although I wish there were five easy steps, it is simpler and harder than that: just one step. I need a new leader; the rest of me will follow. Thankfully, God has provided one in his Holy Spirit and Paul says **"But letting the Spirit control your mind leads to life and peace" (Romans 8:6).**

God knew I would need a new leader, so he provided one. He does not leave us to our own devices; he provides all that we need. This new leader helps us do the right things. Let's keep feeding him!

What I have learned about God so far:

1. He forgives me, he does not condemn me.
2. He leads me and helps me do the right things.

Questions to ask yourself and maybe a trusted friend over coffee:

- Paul says we can think about "sinful things" or we can think about "things that please the Spirit." Which do you think about most?
- What are some "things that please the Spirit?" How do you think you can feed those more?
- What are some things that you think about that might be "sinful things"? How do you think you can avoid them more?

END NOTES:

*Nicholson, Jack. *As Good As It Gets*. Film. Directed by James L. Brooks. Los Angeles: Columbia TriStar Films, 1997.

**Http://basicgoodness.com/2011/the-black-wolf-and-the-white-wolf/

Chapter 3

The Spirit Gives Life

"But you are not controlled by your sinful nature. You are controlled by the Spirit if you have the Spirit of God living in you. (And remember that those who do not have the Spirit of Christ living in them do not belong to him at all.) 10 And Christ lives within you, so even though your body will die because of sin, the Spirit gives you life because you have been made right with God. 11 The Spirit of God, who raised Jesus from the dead, lives in you. And just as God raised Christ Jesus from the dead, he will give life to your mortal bodies by this same Spirit living within you. 12 Therefore, dear brothers and sisters, you have no obligation to do what your sinful nature urges you to do. 13 For if you live by its dictates, you will die. But if through the power of the Spirit you put to death the deeds of your sinful nature, you will live. 14 For all who are led by the Spirit of God are children of God." (Romans 8:9-14)

Have you ever made a choice that you *know* was a dumb one? I know I have. We all make choices. Some are better than others. Some are outright dumb. I believe it is only by God's grace that we have lived through some of our dumb choices. I won't judge your choices, but I will let you judge mine.

I hung around a group of fun-loving guys in high school that we called by the not-so-original name: "the Fellas." We did not party a lot, we did not smoke, we hardly drank, and we stayed away from drugs. We liked to have fun, but not chemically induced fun, if you know what I mean. We played a lot of basketball, we played other sports, we pulled pranks on each other, and we mocked each other on a daily basis. It was all fun; not all of it was smart. One night, we had this bright idea to take our cars out and drive around. It's what bored teenagers did before the internet. At one point, one of the Fellas jumped out of his car, ran over and hit another guy's car, and yelled "you're it!" What happened next is a full-on game of what we later called "bumper tag," where you had to either tap a guy's bumper with your car or get out of your car and go touch the other car. We darted through traffic like a chase scene in one of those *The Fast and the Furious* movies. We cut each other off, we ran each other off the road, and we tapped each other's bumpers just to be able to say we were "not it!" Dumb, right?! ONLY by God's grace were we not hurt and did we not hurt someone else in our antics. In short, we lived to tell about it, dumb as it may have been. **And this should really go without saying but do *not* try this at home!**

Other choices we make can literally be the difference between life and death.

One year after Susie and I were married, we took a trip around the East Coast of the United States. We went to Washington, DC. We went to New York City, Boston, Maine, Niagara Falls, and ended up meeting my brother and his wife in State College, Pennsylvania. We loved the college town. We saw the sights, watched a football practice, and had a nice visit. As part of the jaunt, our hosts had planned a canoe voyage down a lazy river, whose name I have forgotten. We were going to float down the river, meander through the swampy area, and enjoy the slothful summertime afternoon in peace. I had been canoeing a couple of other times in my life, and so had Susie.

While we waited by the side of the slow-moving river, my brother and his wife shuttled the cars so we would have a ride when our journey through down the river was completed. As we waited for our drivers, we talked about our past canoe trips and our river-conquering voyages. What started as sharing ended up as bragging, and devolved into a contest of who would be the better canoer. Although her stories were cute, mine were nothing short of super hero tales, and I had something to prove.

As we started our trek, we put the canoe in the water, pushed it inches into the river, and boarded our vessel. But, as expert canoers should know, if you both get in on the same side and at the same time, you will capsize, and both get wet. Which is what we did. We tried to come aboard at the same time, and we unbalanced the canoe and flipped it right over. I was soaking wet and in knee-deep water when I grabbed the canoe, saving it from taking the trip by itself. I grabbed our stuff and threw it into the canoe when I noticed that Susie was face down in the water, flailing about, and fighting the urge to breathe in water. She was clearly at risk, clearly struggling, and clearly in need of a hero. It was at that split second when I screamed at her these lifesaving words: "Stand up!" She stood up, caught her breath, and has lived happily ever after, other than when I remind her of this story.

Susie had a choice. The choice she made gave her life.

On a much more sobering note, I know that when people get desperate they make choices that can negatively affect their lives and make decisions that will follow them for the rest of their lives. I'll bet that there are some people reading this right now that have dealt with depression or know someone who has. Depression is real and I will deal more in depth with that in chapter 10. I know there are those who have dealt with trauma, abuse, and addicted spouses or parents. I'm sure that these things leave us empty, confused, dead inside, and desperate.

In this section of Romans 8, Paul reminds us that the Spirit *always* gives us life. When we choose to do the things that please God, things that the Spirit is telling us to do, they bring us more life. Those choices bring us up, not down; they give spiritual life and not death.

Jesus himself said that he came to give us life. **"The thief's purpose is to steal and kill and destroy. My purpose is to give them a rich and satisfying life" (John 10:10).** If Jesus' words give us a goal, then Paul gives us the treasure map to follow in order to reach that goal. You want a rich and satisfying life? The Spirit gives us that life.

However, we have an important part in this whole crazy-legged dance. We have free-willed choices to make. The Spirit does not imprison us, hold us against our will in some creepy dungeon, and force his God-centered life on us. After all, would that *really* be the kind of life Jesus promised?! **No, the life Jesus promised, and the Spirit delivers, is one where our choices, our decisions, and our free-will align with God's.** It is a life brought on by ignoring our natural tendencies and surrendering our will to the perfect plan designed by a Perfect Father who wants the best for us. That one choice leads us to a slow dance filled with a lifetime of joy, peace, and grace.

I am not sure about you, but some of my most natural tendencies are not God-honoring in the least. I have a natural tendency to yell at bad drivers, judge people who hurt children, hold a grudge against people who owe me money, get snippy and petty with people who kiss up to the boss, and have an endless supply of exasperation for those in the front of the line in a traffic jam. I mean, can't we all just count to three and press down on the gas pedal? Come on, people! Furthermore, don't even get me started on the choices I would like to make with what to do with people who talk out loud during the movies in the theater.

Being controlled by the Spirit is not some heaven-based puppetry, putting on some cheesy marionette show. It is a voluntary compulsion to do whatever the Spirit leads us to do. However, following God's will for my life *can be* scary, since I am surrendering my control. Right now I am often compelled to do things *my* way. In fact, I have gotten good at tuning God out so that I can do it my way.

Living a God-honoring life means I get compelled to do his will, not mine. In doing so I find that his will gives me real life. And I want *real* life, don't you? **What I have learned about God so far:**

1. He forgives me, he does not condemn me.
2. He leads me and helps me do the right things.
3. He gives us real life.

Questions to ask yourself and maybe a trusted friend over coffee:

- What choices have you made that you regret? What do you think was driving those choices? What do you wish you had done instead?
- Have you ever made choices that you think pleased God? What were they?
- Describe what you think a God-honoring life would look like.
- How would your life look different if you honored God with all of your choices?
- **"But the Holy Spirit produces this kind of fruit in our lives: love, joy, peace, patience, kindness, goodness, faithfulness, gentleness, and self-control. There is no law against these things!" (Galatians 5:22-23)**. Which of these do you feel you need the most? Can you put them in order? What do you think your life would look like right now if you had more of these in your life?
- What do you think God is telling you through this chapter?

Chapter 4

Ever Feel like You Don't Fit In? This May Be Why.

"So you have not received a spirit that makes you fearful slaves. Instead, you received God's Spirit when he adopted you as his own children. Now we call him, "Abba, Father." [16] For his Spirit joins with our spirit to affirm that we are God's children. [17] And since we are his children, we are his heirs. In fact, together with Christ we are heirs of God's glory. But if we are to share his glory, we must also share his suffering." (Romans 8:15-17)

My father was killed when my mother was about seven months pregnant with me. He was electrocuted, but not by the state; I just wanted to clear that up. He was in a freak industrial accident and he was killed instantly by an electrical charge that overwhelmed his body. It left my mother with a four-year-old, a two-year-old, and myself. She had a couple of months before she had to actually deal with a living, breathing, eating, and pooping me, but it was no secret that I was coming.

After the funeral my mom scooped up her little family and took us back to live with her parents in Massachusetts. It is also where my mom worked through her grief over losing her husband. It is where I was born and given my name.

My name is an interesting story. My parents were in church one time when they heard the priest tell the story of Dismas, "the good thief on the cross." When Jesus went to the cross for our sins, he was between two notorious criminals. Sure, Jesus' trial was a sham, but these two other guys legitimately belonged there. On one side of Jesus, a criminal taunted Jesus and tried to goad him by saying that if Jesus was all that, he should get himself off the cross. Although Jesus had the ability to come off the cross, his own stated life's purpose was to die for our sins, so he was not about to give up on that at this point.

On the other side of Jesus was a convicted thief. This guy respected who Jesus was, saw beyond the cross, and asked that Jesus would remember him in paradise. Jesus agreed. A thief, who repented, and was granted a place in heaven by the King of the Jews. He is named as the first saint of the Christian church. It's a great part of the story and a great life lesson: it is never too late to reach out to Jesus.

Although he is not actually named in the Bible, according to Catholic tradition he was named Dismas. My father loved the story, loved the name, and insisted that I be named Dismas Stephen Doherty. He wanted me to walk this planet named Dismas. All I can imagine is the awkward nicknames I would have had: Dizzy, Diz, Christmas, Dismissed, and they could go on and on. Instead, my father died, and my mother's protective wisdom kicked in. She immediately changed the plans and named me Stephen Dismas Doherty. That name stuck. Decades later, people still call me Steve, and only employers, the IRS, and my little sister call me Stephen.

My mother remarried when I was in second grade. Mac was a decent man who loved my mom and her three kids. He also loved his three kids, whom we inherited as step-siblings. In one marriage ceremony I went from being the baby of the family to number five of six. Eventually I was promoted to number five of seven kids. My stepdad (from this point forward I will just call him "dad," which is what I called him throughout my life) and mom decided that they would adopt each other's kids. Apparently when it was time to do so, and since we had dressed up, the judge agreed with them; he probably knew how much work it had been to get all of us looking nice. So, one day in court my identity changed from Stephen Dismas Doherty to Stephen Dismas McNitt. Just like that, I had a new forever name.

However, it turns out Mac loved alcohol more than he loved all of us combined. I am not sure if you have ever dealt with someone who has serious addictions, although statistics would prove that you most likely have. Mac and my mom made things work as best as they could, but the addiction won, as it often does. They divorced when I was in middle school. I learned about their divorce from a friend's mother who read the Public Records in the local newspaper for important news like that. I am not sure which was a bigger shock: my parents were divorced or that I had to hear it from someone else's family?

I mention this to you so that when I said I did not have good role models for how to be a father, I think you will agree. In fact, I was *afraid* to be a father. What positive lessons had I learned? Most of what I had learned about being a dad was from TV; now that should *really* scare you! I had no idea how to swaddle, how to discipline, how to love unconditionally, or how to give wisdom. The only dad thing that I was good at was telling bad jokes.

Those inabilities came up very early in dating Susie, who would later, on some mission of mercy, agree to be my wife. On our second date she asked me what I thought about having kids, which I thought was a little forward, but she knew what future she wanted. I said that I was ambivalent, that I had no positive role models, and that I liked kids but had no idea how to raise them. Susie responded to me in a way that only Susie could: "If you don't know if you want kids, we might want to cut this off right now."

Um, excuse me?!

I was blown away, and it was only our second date. Just to put things in perspective for you, I will let you know that the eHarmony dating website lists second-date questions like: Where is the best place you've traveled to and why would you recommend it? Who in history would you most like to have coffee with? What would be your perfect day? It says *nothing* about "let's have kids or forget it!" Clearly Susie had not read the website details. In her defense, this was before we knew of any websites.

Years later I learned later that my weak response was very nearly the kiss of death in our relationship. **I was not sure**

I wanted kids, but I *was* sure I wanted a lifelong relationship with Susie. I was put on notice from the beginning what her values were and how strongly she felt about having, and raising, children.

After about eighteen months of marriage, we began looking for houses to buy. And, of course, we did have to factor in schools, neighborhoods, and imagine each house as a place to raise kids. It was a bit of a shock to me, being the unsuspecting and oblivious male that I was, and probably still am. Susie wanted us to buy a house on a single income so she could stay home and raise the kids. She would point out the baby's room and where the swing set would go. She could tell which neighbors had little ones, based on the toys in the yard, and the car seat situations. Yes, actually, she was poking around and investigating the neighborhoods as well as the houses.

I was a high school teacher and coach at the time and could not image what kind of dump we would get on my one salary. Again, she was letting me know that children would dominate our goals, our values, our homes, and (this one I got right) our bank accounts. We agreed, but she more avidly supported all of the ideas and consequences of having kids. Susie had always wanted to be a mom. What started out as pretty clear became increasingly *crystal* clear to me. She even let me know that when people asked her, as a child, what she wanted to be when she grew up, she always said "a mom."

Try to imagine the devastation we felt when, after trying to have kids for a year, and trying infertility treatments for another year, we were unable to conceive. In a way, that news seemed so final and so morose to us. The doctor told us "You will never have your own biological children." It wasn't just a gut punch, it was a roundhouse gut punch from Chuck Norris. Because Susie had yearned for this her entire life, it was as if he had told us that Susie had no purpose in life. The cut was so deep and so wide within Susie's soul that I was not sure she would ever recover. The cut was deep in me as well, but I hurt for her more than I grieved the loss of another generation of McNitts. I am a problem solver, a fixer, someone who uses plans, strategies, and connections to make things happen. However, this one I could not fix. This one I could not make better. No amount of connections, resources, or strategies could get us to conceive the child Susie had always wanted.

We took a year to do some counseling, some grieving, and some playing. We imagined our lives without children; I even drove a sports car. We agreed to discuss anything we wanted, but to not make any decisions for a year. The discussions came and went, the grieving continued, and the counseling helped a bunch. In the end we decided to pursue becoming parents through adoption.

It is a shame to fast forward past the selection process to finding the right agency, filling out lots of paperwork, a home study, and some interviews. It was an arduous process, but one that helped us become closer and get us, ever so slightly, more ready to be parents. At one point we were told we were "in the book" and that any birth mom could look at what I called our "baby resume" which explained why we would be great parents. **I *knew* Susie would be a great mom and I hoped I would not cause much damage as a father.** From that point on we were told we could be called at any moment and to be prepared at all times. From that moment on, every phone call we received made our hearts race and our hopes rise. Our instincts became like firefighters who are always ready to grab a bag, jump in their engines, turn up the sirens and lights, and spring into action!

We had months of sitting on the edge of our seats, exhausted waiting, dashed hopes, and angry tirades at telemarketers who had the audacity to call us to sell us vinyl siding when what we *really* wanted was a baby.

Finally, on a Thursday, a woman called from our adoption agency telling me to get home and get on the phone together with Susie so they could tell us all about our new baby. I am sure she had other details, but I am sure I did not hear them or care. We were getting a baby!

Susie and I talked with the social worker, who had some details about the baby, but really we heard only as much as you can when you are in shock. What I mostly thought was "It's go time!" She told us to be at the hospital the next morning to pick up our new son.

We cried. Years of grief were now getting put aside. We laughed at how ridiculously swollen and slobbery we looked as we cried. We panicked and we knew our lives were going to change forever.

When we arrived at the hospital we nervously waited in a designated area for what seemed like a time without end. My nerves were shot, but they took another seismic leap when we were told we could see the baby, our baby. We walked through the lobby, down a seemingly endless corridor past a window where you could see all the babies. The nurse motioned us to go around the corner to a window only big enough for Susie and I to look through. The nurse inside rolled a hospital crib thingy over to us and gave us the thumbs up sign; laying there was our baby boy. We named him Noah.

I remember every detail of that timeless moment. I remember holding Susie and looking at this little blanketed bundle with a perfectly round face sticking out. I remember that we had anticipated that moment for years and that Noah slept right through it. I remember that as Susie and I looked at that perfect baby-clad bundle of sleep that we released years of stress, years of grief, a lifetime of joy, and about six gallons of tears. We cried so hard our bodies were heaving and our joy had overwhelmed us. In that moment our identities changed; we became parents. Although it would take months for the legalities to play out, in that moment Noah joined our family tree, family will, family vacations, and family pictures forever.

I wonder, to this day, if that is the same reaction God has when one of us comes into a relationship with him. In Luke's gospel he tells three stories of people who lose something very important to them and the joy they feel when that lost thing is finally found. There is a lost coin, lost sheep, and lost son. He goes on to say "**there is joy in the presence of God's angels when even one sinner repents" (Luke 15:10).** In other words, the angels in heaven rejoice and party when even one soul has come to Jesus. I imagine a massive, standing-room-only party arena where they are watching a big-screen TV. When someone gives their life to God, the arena erupts in this kind of sobbing, heaving, joyful celebration after years of hoping and praying for us to get right with God. The writer of the Book of Hebrews says that "**we are surrounded by such a huge crowd of witnesses to the life of faith" (Hebrews 12:1)** who are cheering for us.

The adoptions of each of our boys were special. The stories could not be more different, but the results were the same. In the end, both boys joined our family and have been important and special parts ever since. Both boys have our last name. Both boys are in our will as equal shares, despite my tongue-in-cheek threats to the contrary. Both boys are fully, legally part of our family, and nothing will ever change that.

I hope you can get what Paul says to us in Romans 8 that we are *adopted* into God's family. We get to be fully included into his future, his plans, and full heirs with Jesus. By now I hope you know how much God loves his son Jesus. Here Paul tells us that we can be adopted into God's family, just like that!

Do you ever wonder why you feel left out? Do you ever wonder where you belong? **If you follow Jesus, you belong in the family of God as a fully adopted member. You are not a stepchild!** You are not some kid that hangs around the house enough that they treat you "like one of the family." Sometimes you hear about some rich people who leave an inheritance to some distant nephew because they did not have kids of their own. That is *not* you! *You* are a treasured child of the Most High God! Our adoption is affirmed by the Holy Spirit in a way that we may never feel like we belong to any other family, we may never feel like we fit in anywhere else. Sometimes in life we struggle and try and fit in some places, with some groups, trying different groups, or friends. It may feel awkward, because where you are meant to fit in is within the loving embrace of your Heavenly Father, the God Almighty.

Sometimes when we feel like outsiders, it feels like we just don't know who we are. After all, it is impossible to know *who* you are until you know *whose* you are. God made you. God designed you in a special, unique, and purposeful way. God sent his only Son to give his life to repair our relationship with him. God is awaiting a telephone call, text, Snap Chat, or some other way to say that there is a new child awaiting him, and that child is *you*! Our loving, perfect Heavenly Father adopts you with no strings attached. Your adoption is forever. God's adoption of you is, literally, forever. It is ceaseless, timeless, unending, everlasting, and eternal. At the moment that Susie and I adopted Noah, nothing else mattered. We were not thinking about the fertility treatments, the waiting, the disappointments, or any hassles in the timing of the process. When they placed Noah in our arms it did not matter that we were not the birth parents; what mattered was that we were *his* parents. We knew he was our child, forever. This is how it is with God. We are adopted into his kingdom and his family. Just as we *knew* we were Noah's parents, we should *know* that we belong to our Heavenly Father.

He loves you and he includes you.
THIS is where you fit in!
Paul says in this section that "**...you received God's Spirit when he adopted you as his own children. Now we call him, 'Abba, Father'" (Romans 8:15).** When we belong to him, we are fully adopted and fully inherit his kingdom, his riches, his heaven, his love, his commitment, and his Spirit.

Knowing that the God of the Universe, the Most High, and the Everlasting (his titles go on and on!) wanted to adopt me was overwhelming. It was mind-blowing. And it was too good to pass up, and so I decided to follow Jesus and join God's family when I was fifteen years old. I have never regretted it. It has made my life better, my character better, and given me a most amazing hope for my future on earth and my eternal future connected to the most loving and perfect father there is.

I am a treasured and beloved child of the Most High God. And if you follow Jesus, so are you. It is who you are and whose you are. No matter what you think, how you feel or what others tell you, your adoption is final.

Not to rain on the parade, but I feel like I would not be keeping it real unless I gave you two bits of warning at this point. The first is that you are not the only one adopted into this family, and wherever there are people there will be irritating people. So, like all families, in God's family there are dysfunctional and irritating people. Sorry about that; it just is what it is. Like every family, there are good times, bad times, joy, and sadness. In God's family you get both, but in the end the promises of a perfect eternity might help you endure the less-than-perfect family that is stuck here on earth for now.

The second warning is this: you can *only* get into God's family through adoption. There are no natural childbirths in this family. It does not matter what your parents or grandparents do; *you* only get in through adoption. The great thing about this is that you do not get any of the blame for any knuckleheads in your earthly family, and you do not get excluded because of any knucklehead stuff you have done in your past (see Romans 8:1). This is all on you. You get to decide whether to follow Jesus or not. You get to decide whether you are adopted or not. You get to decide how much of your love, your life, your heart, your mind, your strength, and your soul you will give to God. He wants it all; you decide what he gets.

He has already decided to love you. Just as Susie and I were waiting for a call from our adoption agency to say we had a son, he is just waiting for the call that you are joining his family. And if you never have before, what are you waiting for? A simple prayer like this one can get this family party started: "Jesus, thank you for loving me even when I don't deserve it. Thank you for coming to me and offering to adopt me into your family. I want to be part of your family, but I have done things that have not made you proud. Please forgive me for those things and please adopt me into your family. I will love you and allow you to be my leader. Amen."

If you prayed a prayer like that just now, or any time in your past, then thank you for reading onward, my family member! I will see you at the family reunion, if not sooner. Remember that if you are ever confused about your identity or if you ever get confused about where you fit in, that this is true: **God's family is where you will completely fit in, forever.**

What I have learned about God so far:

1. He forgives me, he does not condemn me.
2. He leads me and helps me do the right things.
3. He gives us real life.
4. He adopts me into his family.

Questions to ask yourself and maybe a trusted friend over coffee:

- What is your earthly family like? What things make them awesome? Awful? Different from other families?
- What do you think it was like when you were adopted into God's family?
- Do you have anyone on earth who loves you totally, even if that person may not have liked every choice you have made?
- What do you think it means to be part of God's family?
    - What kinds of things do you think God wants from his family members?

Chapter 5

God's Glory > Our Suffering

**"Yet what we suffer now is nothing compared to the
glory he will reveal to us later. 19 For all creation is
waiting eagerly for that future day when God will reveal
who his children really are. 20 Against its will, all creation
was subjected to God's curse. But with eager hope, 21 the
creation looks forward to the day when it will join God's
children in glorious freedom from death and decay."
(Romans 8:18-21)**

I love sports. I love all different kinds of sports. Sports are the first, and still the best, reality TV. Sports bring the thrill of victory and the agony of defeat. They are a little slice of human drama right in front of you. I love to play sports, watch sports, and on most mornings you will catch me listening to sports talk radio on my commute to work. I love the competition; I love the athletes pushing themselves to be better and to be excellent in the midst of hard circumstances. I know that at the end of the day you can push yourself so hard, yet come up short on the outcome, but I still love the struggle and the competition of sports.

When I was younger I played linebacker and center on my high school football team, threw the shot for the track team, and wrestled for my high school team. I was not great, but I won some and I lost some. I have great memories of teams I have been on, the lessons I have learned, and the friendships I have made. I have memories of the shots I have made on the basketball court and how I used to be able to jump high enough to touch the ten-foot rim. I remember an interception I made in a football game, followed by a tackle by the opposing quarterback that knocked the wind out of me. I have special memories of being on a wrestling mat, challenging my body and mind and getting someone into a hold and getting to pin them to the mat, then shaking hands and being friends afterwards.

Ever since I was much younger, I have loved the discussions that happen around sports. I love that we can talk all day about games, records, and players. I love that we passionately argue that our favorite player or team is the greatest. At the end of the day it is about comparing different things. Although players may play the same position, if they are from different eras those can be completely different discussions. For instance, many people think Babe Ruth is the greatest baseball player ever. However, he did not play in an era when baseball was integrated, so he was not playing against the best athletes, only the best white athletes. So, was he really better than Sachel Paige, a star in the Negro League?

I especially like the discussions about who is the greatest (fill in the blank). Who is the greatest Dodger player? Who is the greatest basketball player? Who is the greatest player ever to wear number 33? I think it is Kareem Abdul-Jabbar, the leading scorer in NBA history, and I will argue with you all night if I have to. However, just saying that will get me into arguments with fans of Larry Bird. I love when we discuss the greatest sports records ever made. I think it is that Wilt Chamberlain played thirteen seasons and never fouled out; he was available whenever you needed him. It might also be that he scored 100 points in a game, I don't think we will see that one broken. I would also entertain that Cal Ripken Jr. played in 2,632 games consecutively, which is pretty amazing to play that many games and never get hurt or get the flu or get tired of showing up. He broke the previous record by over 500 games. With all the major league players wanting rest these days, it does not seem likely we will see that equaled anytime soon.

I love the comparison discussions. I think lots of people like to compare. When I watch the Oscars on TV, it seems like the commentators are comparing her dress to that other lady's dress. They are comparing this one's acting role to the role he played last year when he was *not* nominated.

My wife has been a teacher for over twenty years, mostly to kindergartners. It is amazing the stories she brings home of parents who are comparing their child to the classroom norm. They want to see where their kid lines up against the competition. They will also compare this child to their older sibling. The comparisons seem to roll off their tongues like it is their native language. There is a norm for height, weight, reading levels, and politeness. Every parent wants to know that their kid is normal, or better than normal. Meanwhile, every teenager wants to know if they have had more likes on their Instagram account than they did on their post yesterday. Most teens know how many followers they have on Twitter, Facebook, or Instagram and they compare that to each other's followers.

If you are around old people long enough, they will tell stories comparing their lives to how easy the younger generation has it. Which reminds me, when I was young I had to walk to school five miles each way, in the snow. It snowed a lot more in Southern California back then. The walk was not that bad if it was your day to wear the family pair of shoes! We older folks can compare our health issues to one another. My mother's husband, Jim Morgan, used to call it the organ recital: "my lungs are clogged, my liver is acting up, my heart stopped twice today..."

There are difficult comparisons, too. Many of us compare our pain to one another's. As a therapist, I have had people tell me about their awful childhoods in such explicit and nauseating detail as a way to clue me into their beliefs that their pain was much worse than mine. Undoubtedly they do this before ever hearing my story. I have had people show me especially icky scars just so they could tell me the story behind their hideous injuries. Rarely have I heard people bragging about their childhood as a way to explain how much *better* it was than mine. We just love to compare, don't we?!

When people compare their pain it is because they are still feeling the ripples from that pain. I have a son who has had leukemia twice. To me it is the most difficult thing I have ever been through; it is a 10 out of 10 on my pain scale. But others will look at the death of their loved one and count that as a 10. Some people experience divorce as a 10, and others remember their abuse as a 10. A teenager may experience the loss of their first love as a 10. Can they all be tens? Of course they can. **We experience pain only as it relates to us, so our worst will be a 10. Everyone else's worst will be a 10 to them, too.** It does not matter if it is being dumped by our first love, being turned down for a prom date, an irritating hangnail, or having a loved one die unexpectedly. Each can be 10 to us in that moment, based on our personal life experience.

In this section of Romans 8, the Apostle Paul compares our current pains with the future glory of the Lord. Well, I guess technically he says there is *no* comparing the two. He says that we all are looking forward to when God's glory is clear to us, when we no longer have to have these bodies and when it will be so awesome we will forget our painful pasts. **He is giving us a hint that if our pain is a 10 now, then God's glory will be a 10 bazillion in the other direction! Our pain is real, it is intense, and it can define us, but by God's measuring stick it is a pebble to step over, and our future with God is a Mount Everest of awesome, eye-popping love, joy, grace, and acceptance.**

This is a theme we see throughout the Bible. In the Old Testament, the story of Job's life starts out as amazing: he has a wife, riches, children, land, and lots of animals while being remarkably faithful to God. His life takes an awful turn when he loses his children, his animals, and his riches all in one day. His wife remains by his side, but in a cruel twist of irony she is a complete downer. She sees his misery; after all, she is sharing in it. She comes to him in the lowest moment of his life and **"His wife said to him, 'Are you still trying to maintain your integrity? Curse God and die'" (Job 2:9).** How is that for the supportive wife? I mean WOW! She just lays it out there in the extreme: curse God and die. No flowery sayings, no positive memes, or sugar-coating things for her. It gets somewhat better when his friends come alongside him. They remain silent for a week, which seems helpful. When they finally talk, they spend the next sixteen chapters arguing with Job about all that he has done wrong in his life, that God has abandoned him, and that he has no right to be faithful.

Through Job's miserable and traumatic journey he remains heroically faithful to God and tells his friends: **"But as for me, I *know* that my Redeemer lives, and *he will* stand upon the earth at last. 26 And after my body has decayed, yet in my body *I will* see God! 27 *I will* see**

him for myself. Yes, *I will* see him with my own eyes. I am overwhelmed at the thought!" (Job 19:25-27) Job remains faithful because his is *convinced* that God would remain faithful to him. Job has every right to be ticked off at God, to turn his back on God, and reject God. He has every right except one: God has not abandoned him. God is still with him and God has promised to be faithful.

In Romans 8 Paul is convinced in the same way that our current problems will be *nothing* compared to the greatness of God's glory! Paul and Job knew deep in their hearts that our best days are ahead of us. They knew that God had not let them down, even though you couldn't tell it at the very moment when those words were written.

After all, Job lost most every material thing within his reach and Paul was writing his letter from a prison cell. At the moment that these were written, it looked like both of their lives stunk, to everyone but Paul and Job. They both knew that they could easily endure their current circumstances because they had their eyes on the future prize. They knew that this world is not all there is. They knew that what they endured at the time would be bad, but what they got to have later would be 10 bazillion times better!

In fact, God's awesome future is a theme throughout the Bible. One of my favorite spots comes in the last book, the next-to-the-last chapter. The Apostle John gets some sneak previews of what heaven will be like: **"I heard a loud shout from the throne, saying, 'Look, God's home is now among his people! He will live with them, and they will be his people. God *himself* will be with them. [4] He will wipe every tear from their eyes, and there will be no more death or sorrow or crying or pain. All these things are gone forever.' [5] And the one sitting on the throne said, 'Look, I am making everything new!'" (Revelation 21:3-5)**

If that does not seem awesome to you, you might be reading it wrong. Try it again, only slower; can you see it? Can you imagine it? You might need to read it again and again; I know I did. I read it until I could wrap my mind around what it would look like. Can you see it? Keep looking, because it is beautiful! **Imagine the place where there is no more death or sorrow or crying or pain, and we will live in that place forever. I don't know about you, but my life has had more than enough death, pain, sorrow, and tears.** I don't need any more, thank you. I think I have seen enough of that for one lifetime.

I imagine heaven as this: instead of hospitals there are hiking trails and parks where all of us healthy people live, play, and enjoy the company of our loved ones, new and old. Instead of mortuaries there are gyms where we exercise our new bodies while the staff keeps us hydrated with milk to go with our warm chocolate chip cookies. There are scales there that prove we have not gained a pound. Instead of numbers on the scale it has only words that say things like "you are loved for who you are, not what you weigh" and "what do you care, you are a beloved child of the Most High God!" Instead of Kleenex that is intended you wipe your tears of sadness, people lend you their sleeves to wipe your tears of joy, your tears that came from laughing too hard, and your tears of gratitude to a God who has redeemed your life, your relationships, and your very soul.

Can you see it? A place where God has made *everything* new. There are new rules based on security, love, and being fully, permanently, and ultimately satisfied. We have new relationships based on honesty, respect, and purity. New cultural norms are based on relating to a God who loves us and always will. Everything is new. The old is gone. All things are new, complete, and perfectly done in a way to honor God, which also honors others, and honors ourselves.

I know there are many people reading this who are going through pain and would love to just shout at me, "you don't know what I am going through." I know there are those who want to keep reminding others that our current life is real and can be painful, and that we endure pain and threats of harm every day. We live in a world with diseases, power struggles, wars, human trafficking, abuse, cancers, hate, violence, racism, school shootings, and other horrors. Yet, *none* of this is a surprise to our Heavenly Father. *None* of this is unexpected, and he has prepared a better future for us. God has prepared us something so great it seems dumb to even compare it to the broken place we currently call home.

God is in control. **God's future will be so amazing it doesn't even compare to what we already know so well.** Yes, friends, our best days are ahead of us, so hang on for the ride.

One last thought about hanging on. We can do anything for a while, right? I mean we endure the unmentionable pain and humility of the dentist's chair, but only for a while. No one could get their teeth scraped with a metal hook every day. When we have the urge to go to the bathroom, we can hold it, but only for a little while. You can hold it longer if you do a little dance, hop around, or force your knees together; but even that is temporary. When we have a nagging little brother or an irritating little sister, we can put up with it, but not forever. At some point we will have to do something else to ease the pain, or we hope they grow up to be less irritating.

I have read stories of people doing amazing feats of endurance. I saw a movie once about people running the Western States 100-mile footrace. It goes through the Sierra Nevada Mountains and ends on a high school track. I don't know how they do it, and even more puzzling is *why* they do it. After all, the prize is a belt buckle. That's not for me, besides, my belt already has a buckle. I read a story about David Blaine, who lived in an icebox in Times Square, New York, for almost sixty-four hours, enduring freezing temperatures, sleep deprivation, and the people scratching their heads and wondering why.

In the midst of every endurance event there comes a time when you have to ask yourself *why* you are laboring on. In those moments of self-doubt, if you don't know why you are doing something, you will find reasons, among the discouragement, to quit. If you are going to follow a task all the way to the end, you will need to know why you are doing it to begin with.

It is the reason I never learned to juggle. I tried a few times; I watched some videos, I got some bean bags, and I practiced against a wall. I did everything the jugglers told me. However, at the end of the day it was juggling. And juggling may be cool to watch for a minute or two, but I just wasn't into it enough to keep practicing. The practicing was hard, and it got frustrating and I did not have enough of a "why" to keep up the hard work. So I quit. If you don't know why you are doing something, you will quit too.

I think God knew that, and Paul recognized that too. So they gave us the "why" in what today would be printed in all caps! Why should we endure the ugly, scarring, brutal realities of this world? Because they are **"nothing compared to the glory he will reveal to us later."** The breathtaking, unbelievable, fantastic, and grace-filled future with God will outshine this world by 10 bazillion. What a remarkable future to look forward to. So hang in there: our best days are ahead. In our future days, our Heavenly Father himself will wipe your tears. There will be no more grief from friends and family passing before us. We will have no crying and no pain. And best of all it will be that way incessantly, permanently, perpetually, and eternally.

God thinks, and I think, you can hang in there for all of that. When you do, he promises that your best days are ahead of you!

What I have learned about God so far:

1. He forgives me, he does not condemn me.
2. He leads me and helps me do the right things.
3. He gives us real life.
4. He adopts me into his family.
5. If I follow God, my best days are ahead of me.

Questions to ask yourself and maybe a trusted friend over coffee:

- What is something you do better than some people? What is something you wish you were better at?
- What are some hard things you have been through?
- When you think of the hard things in your life, which are the 10's? How have they affected you and your identity?
- What are some things you wish God would do for you?
- What things have caused you pain? Sorrow? Tears? What would life be like without those things in your life?
- If your best days are really ahead of you, what do you hope that will include?
- What are some things you hope will happen in heaven? Why?

Chapter 6

There *Is* Hope and I'll Bet You Feel It

"For we know that all creation has been groaning as in the pains of childbirth right up to the present time.
23 And we believers also groan, even though we have the Holy Spirit within us as a foretaste of future glory, for we long for our bodies to be released from sin and suffering. We, too, wait with eager hope for the day when God will give us our full rights as his adopted children, including
the new bodies he has promised us. 24 We were given
this hope when we were saved. (If we already have
something, we don't need to hope for it. 25 But if we look
forward to something we don't yet have, we must wait patiently and confidently.)" (Romans 8:22-25)

It has been said that a person can live for forty days without food, seven days without water, but not a minute without hope. **Hope gives life, saves lives, and creates purpose in your life.** The version of the Bible I am using for this book (New Living Translation) mentions hope *190 times*. Surprisingly, grace is only mentioned 95 times. Based just on that alone, I would call hope a significant theme that is sprinkled throughout the Bible. In the most famous Bible passage about love, Paul writes that **"Three things will last forever—faith, hope, and love—and the greatest of these is love." (1 Corinthians 13:13)** Hope makes it into his top three things in life. I wonder if you would agree with how important hope is to our lives?

A Google search for quotes about hope gave 31.8 million results. Goodreads had 11,961 hope quotes on its site. One of their first entries* was this famous song lyric in a classic song about envisioning a better world in our future: **"You may say I'm a dreamer, but I'm not the only one. I hope someday you'll join us. And the world will live as one." – John Lennon ("Imagine").**

In our lives we have all hoped for many things:

> I hope I can get a Caramel Macchiato.
> I hope the teacher does not collect the homework.
> I am about to propose marriage to my girlfriend; I hope she says yes.
> I hope Mom does not find out.
> I hope that Jimmy likes me back.
> I hope the biopsy is negative.

I hope I have enough in my account to cover this bill.
I hope there is air in the spare tire.
I hope I can lose twenty-five pounds by tomorrow.
I hope the delivery is fast and the baby is healthy.
I hope I get this job.
I hope he can quit drinking forever this time.
I hope our daughter returns from the war.
I hope the hurricane misses our house.
I hope Grandpa remembers me today.

So many parts of our lives are bathed in hope; it drives so much of our thoughts, our prayers, and our nail-biting. Often a glimmer of hope drives us to our knees in prayer, looking for a listening God who will grant us our wishes. Sometimes we hope that we can find support, likes, and answers on our Facebook account, our Twitter, email, and Snap Chat in times of need. In other words, hope sometimes twists our minds slightly into some delusional belief that we have a chance of having things work out. All you have to do is look at the popular chain letters or pyramid schemes to see how much hope some people put in circumstances to pull us through. Do those ever work?

Often the things that we hope for will work out, but sometimes they do not. You see, when we lose hope we get, you know, hopeless. Hopelessness is the root of so many kinds of anxiety and depression. When people have nothing to believe in, nothing to hope for, nothing to look forward to, they easily become despondent. If you have seen the news headlines recently you might think that we live in hopeless times. The Old Testament prophet Amos said that it might even get worse as time goes on: **"In that day you will be like a man who runs from a lion—only to meet a bear. Escaping from the bear, he leans his hand against a wall in his house—and he's bitten by a snake. Yes, the day of the LORD will be dark and hopeless, without a ray of joy or hope" (Amos 5:19,20).** How is that for depressing? Not even a *single* ray of hope is given.

Have you ever felt like that? One thing after another is going wrong; when it rains, it pours. It is in those moments when we feel at our rock bottom, lower than low, and most hopeless, praying that the tide will turn soon. In times like that, some people even become suicidal. In fact, most people have had suicidal thoughts at one time or another. I had a professor in graduate school who said that people become suicidal when they feel hopeless, helpless, and worthless. It is in that wasteland of despair, that journey bereft of hope, that life feels so dismal. Some of you reading this know exactly what I mean because you are in it right now. Many of us have had seasons where we could not imagine a better future. Many of us have had sleepless nights where we did not know *what* we would do next, and every choice seemed horribly bad.

Impossibility is rooted in our fears; hope grows from our faith.

Our Heavenly Father *always* wants us to have faith, hope, and love. He provides sacred pathways to get our relationship right with him. Into a hopeless world he sent his Son, Jesus, as a beacon of hope and light. The ancient world was overflowing with corruption, slavery, male-dominated laws, abject poverty, and chronic chaos. Yet, into that hopeless abyss of humanity stepped God into a bod: Jesus. It was into that dark place that Jesus brought the hopeful news that we could, once again, have a right and true relationship with God. Although we often turn our backs on God, although we have sinned, although we have tried to do life our own way and not his, we can be right with God.

Earlier in his letter to the Romans, Paul said **"But God showed his great love for us by sending Christ to die for us while we were still sinners" (Romans 5:8).** Even while we were rebellious, self-serving, self-seeking sinners, God sent Jesus down to save us from ourselves, our urges, and our worst decisions. We, who follow Jesus, are saved from our sins through the grace and power of Jesus Christ.

Paul is so clear here that we can wait for new bodies, new roles, and a new way of living; we have reason to hope that the best days are ahead of us! Paul says, "**we long for our bodies to be released from sin and suffering. We, too, wait with eager *hope* for the day when God will give us our full rights as his adopted children, including the new bodies he has promised us. We were given this *hope* when we were saved" (Romans 8:23b, 24).**

We found this verse to be such a rich fountain of blessing for us in our family's past. My son, Caleb, had leukemia, went into remission and remained cancer-free for three years and 12 days. When he relapsed he needed a bone marrow transplant. We had hope that his bone marrow transplant would give him a new body, free from cancer, free from the worry of death, and free to grow up into a loving and happy young man. We found hope in so many places, but especially thinking that Caleb's best days were ahead of him.

God-guided hope can be powerful, reassuring, soothing, motivating, and prevailing. Can you feel it? I know I can. I feel the relentless hope that God will redeem us once again, that we will have new bodies, and we will feel included through adoption into God's forever family. I feel confident that we will be released from our current suffering, from the suffering around us, from our sins, and the consequences that swim around us carried with other people's sin. We can have hope again.

It is hard to have hope in the governments that have created the problems of this world. It is hard to continue to hope in the things we buy, vacations we take, or in companies that promise us thinner, prettier bodies, and with environmental-friendly packaging. It is hard to hope in the relationships when the result is pain or back-stabbing. It is hard to believe in the goodness of civilization when we watch the evil in every newscast, where people not only act uncivilized, but cruel.

We all feel that things are not right in this world. We know that humans were made to love puppies more than to fight wars. We know that people were made for the community we feel at a barbecue with friends, not begging on street corners for our basic needs. We know that we were made more for laughter than for misery. We know that we were made to be close to God, not feeling alone and abandoned by him. We feel it in our core, and we often scratch our heads when we hear of increasing evil acts, school shootings, car bombings, shaken babies, tortured puppies, and increasing sex slave trade. We join the human chorus that screams, "What is *wrong* with people?"

Collectively we all long for more goodness, light, and hope. We were built to hope. It is only when we are let down or damaged that we give up hope, if only to protect our feelings and our spirit. Nevertheless, God still moves in our world, right here, right now. When Caleb was sick we asked God for healing, for a bone-marrow donor, for the treatments to work out in our favor; and they did, right before our very own eyes. Into this world God gives us the hope of salvation, the hope of a better future, the hope of adoption, the hope of forgiveness, the hope of community, and the hope of a loving Father who will not abandon us, harm us, or misuse us. He gives us hope, through our faith and his love; right here, right now.

There is hope readily available to us, and I optimistically think you feel it, and so does God. **You see, the forces in our world that intend for us to lose hope are not *ever, ever, ever, ever, ever, ever* from our loving God.** Our God promises us new bodies, a new forever family, new freedom from sin and suffering. He is waiting for us to join him when we will fully experience his love, his community, and his miraculous grace. Yes, our best days are ahead of us and I hope you feel it. In fact, I know you do somewhere inside. It may come as a warm feeling when you worship God, or in an emptiness that you have not been able to fill yet. Either way, it is a sign that there is something more awaiting you.

I know it is coming; God has promised.

What I have learned about God so far:

1. He forgives me, he does not condemn me.
2. He equips me and helps me do the right things.
3. He gives us real life.
4. He adopts me into his family.
5. If I follow God, my best days are ahead of me.
6. He gives me hope, and I *really* always need hope.

Questions to ask yourself and maybe a trusted friend over coffee:

- Do you ever feel hopeless or helpless?
- What are the things that make you feel the happiest?
- What are your hopes for the future? What do you think will help make those happen? What are the things you think are the hurdles that could keep those hopes from happening?
- What are the things you think God hopes for you?
- What do you hope will happen for the people you love the most?

Endnotes:

*https://www.goodreads.com/quotes/tag/hope

Chapter 7

Prayer 101

"And the Holy Spirit helps us in our weakness. For example, we don't know what God wants us to pray for. But the Holy Spirit prays for us with groanings that cannot be expressed in words. [27] And the Father who knows all hearts knows what the Spirit is saying, for the Spirit pleads for us believers in harmony with God's own will." (Romans 8:26, 27)

I have a lot of friends who love sports; they love to watch sports, love to play sports, love to coach sports, and some are owners of their very own fantasy sports teams. Sports are a big part of their lives. The more they know about sports, the more they listen to sports talk radio, the more they listen to knowledgeable broadcasters, the more they think they understand the nuances of their beloved sports. They are self-ordained experts, "whizzes of wonder," and as my friend Danny used to say, "a legend in their own shower." With great authority comes great responsibility. So, if you are watching a game with them in the comfort of your home or theirs, they will regale you with flowery commentary, sometimes in salty language not even a sailor should hear. They spend extended time shouting at their television set, tablet, or other device at the top of their lungs as if their outcries could change the outcome of the game. They will yell at the coach, the players, the announcers, other fans and, of course, the referees. Nonetheless, those on the receiving end of that yelling never seem to turn to the camera and yell back. It's as if they cannot even hear my friends yelling at them. Weird. It never seems to bother my friends. They are patiently relentless in their commentary, criticisms, and cracking me up.

When it comes to prayer, a lot of us can relate to that description. A lot of us feel like we talk to God, yell at God, plead with God, and even just speak to God; but he never looks at the camera and talks back. It's as if he cannot hear us; but we don't think that is weird, do we? In fact, most of us have become unconsciously accustomed to it and don't expect it to be any different. In fact, if we did hear from God we would think we were going insane, like the bag lady near the market who sometimes looks like she is losing an argument to herself.

However, God has always intended prayer to be more. **In fact, God still speaks; and we get to listen.** Most people I know are not great listeners, and that might be the *real* problem with prayer. We may doubt God's intentional connection with us, but he *is* speaking. If we are not hearing him, or if we doubt we are hearing him, here are a few good questions to ask yourself: Are you listening? Do you give God the time and space to block everything else out and really intently listen? Are you waiting quietly and expectantly for him to speak, guide, and encourage you? In other words, do you *really* expect answers?

I have known so many people over the years who will tell me that they are just waiting for an answer from God and they become paralyzed and cannot move until they hear from him. However, you can't drive a parked car. Generally those people are asking for where to work, who to date, and who to marry, for example. I know God speaks in those areas too, but his main concerns are for our own spiritual development and growth. In other words, I think he cares more about who we are becoming than he does who we date or where we work. On a side note: who you date will most definitely influence who you are becoming, so it is a really good idea to pray about that.

In this section of Romans 8, Paul gets at a fundamental truth: **"we don't know what God wants us to pray for"**

(Romans 8:26). If we were honest we might agree that it is tough to know what God wants from us or what we are even supposed to pray. What a lost and hopeless feeling. Unfortunately, it is way too common a feeling among the people I know. I am *sure* that God wants more for our communication; I got that idea from Paul. You see, it is the Holy Spirit's full-time job to be praying for us! He's not just praying random stuff for us; he is praying **"in harmony with God's own will" (Romans 8:27).** What a completely amazing thing this is; we have someone praying for us full time, praying right on point with God's will, and someone God trusts, knows, and answers.

Have you ever prayed for a friend or relative who was troubled?

> You were joining the efforts of the Holy Spirit, who is praying that same thing.

Did you ever pray to get closer to God?

> He prayed that too, probably before you did.

Pray for a relationship?

> Check.

Pray for health and healing?

> Done.

Pray for forgiveness?

Yep.

Pray for wisdom?

Way ahead of you.

Pray for God's grace and mercy?

Of course.

Not sure *what* to pray?

He's there with you in that, too.

Pray for someone else to get struck down by God's almighty wrath?

Uh, you might be on your own there. He's probably not into that one, sorry.

You see, he will pray for you **"in harmony with God's own will."** He will not, however, grant us all of our self-centered wishes like some celestial vending machine. **He will teach us to pray, pray on our behalf, pray according to God's will, pray in ways we might not understand, but he will not be our puppet and do our will, only God's.**

To be honest, that has ticked me off sometimes! My prayers go to God, and he is supposed to give me good things, right? I think all the things I want are good things. So he should give me what I want, right? I mean I want what I want. When my wants, my desires, my hopes are different from God's, I try to angle for it, manipulate it, argue for it, or just *really* try to get God to see my logic. Only, he's God and I am not. He knows better than I do what I need. I usually only know what I want.

So let me give you a list of ways I have tried to manipulate God, and maybe you can relate. Thankfully he sees right through my manipulating garbage.

> "God, if I am a good person and I pray for what I want, I should get it, right?!"

> "God, you want me to be happy, right?"

> "I just feel so sure that ____________ (the thing I want) must be God's will, but it is not happening right now. What's wrong?"

> "God, if you help me pass this test, I will give up ____________________ (whatever bad habit I am working on at the time)."

Thankfully, the Almighty God does not bend and sway like the people we can manipulate or guilt into doing stuff for us. Our God has a perfect and holy will for us and for our lives. He is hoping we get there and that we spend most of our lives enveloped by it. The Holy Spirit even prays for us when we are wandering off from his will or wondering about it. God does not change his will for us so that we will have a temporary happy feeling. He's better than that.

God cares most about our character, our spiritual growth, our integrity, our ability to love him, and love people. God is so completely focused on those things and he knows we will struggle with all of them. So he sent us a helper, a counselor, the Holy Spirit to pray for us and to help us pray when we are not sure how. Could you use a prayer helper? I know I can.

When my wife and I got married, we used to like to take car trips. In fact, we still do. In the early years we would go to the AAA club, get a map, and figure out how to get there (for you young people who don't know what a map is, Google it, they used to come already printed out). One time we were in San Francisco, trying to locate a bed and breakfast inn where we were going to spend a couple of nights. That city has a lot of one-way streets. Some areas, like the one where we were going, seemed to *only* have one-way streets. On this particular day there were also oodles of construction sites, closed streets, and detours. If you live in a city, a detour is just that; if you are a tourist, a detour is a highly disappointing roadblock, like a moat that seems impenetrable at the time. You finally get near your destination only to be denied. It is a lot like when you were a kid, if you waited to open your biggest Christmas gift last only to find out it is underwear or socks.

This particular trip tested our patience and grace like nothing else. It was as if we were circling our destination, not able to get there, and the construction sites just mocked our navigational inabilities. After what seemed like an hour of yelling, re-routing, and refusing to ask directions, we made our destination; we were angry but we were there. We never asked for help. We arrived, worn out, and had worn out each other's last good nerves.

Fast forward to last weekend, thirty-ish years later. We went to a town we do not know very well for the weekend. This time when we got lost, we turned on our global positioning system (GPS), and it re-routed us easily, spoke to us nicely, and we arrived at a lovely wedding in a good mood and had a wonderful night. I am not sure how a GPS works, but it seems to connect with a satellite, sift through lots of data, plan ahead for roadblocks, and get you to the right place. We could have taken any directions we wanted, but when we listened to the helper we arrived at our destination unhurried and unscathed.

The Holy Spirit sometimes acts like a prayer-empowered GPS. He checks in with a higher power, and knows your spiritual, and character, whereabouts. He takes in all the dangers and roadblocks around you and helps you get right into the middle of God's will and get you to your destination. The Holy Spirit is not a replacement for prayer. He is an aide, a helper, and an advocate. We can talk to God, we can listen, and we can get help. Our prayer guarantees a connection to God. Listening to the Holy Spirit guarantees we are headed the right way and will arrive in the right spot, at the right time, and for the right reasons.

Should we talk to God? Absolutely.
Does he communicate back? Absolutely.
Can we get help when we need it? Absolutely.

What I have learned about God so far:

1. He forgives me, he does not condemn me.
2. He equips me and helps me do the right things.
3. He gives us real life.
4. He adopts me into his family.
5. If I follow God, my best days are ahead of me.
6. He gives me hope, and I really need hope.
7. I can talk to him, he will talk to me, and I can get his holy help.

Questions to ask yourself and maybe a trusted friend over coffee:

- How often do you pray?
- Have you ever had a prayer that was answered? What was that like for you?
- Have you ever prayed for something and felt like it went unanswered? How did you deal with that? Why do you think God does that sometimes?
- What do you think your prayers sound like on the receiving end? In other words, what do you think God hears from you?
- What is it like to know that you have a helper, an advocate, a counselor in the Holy Spirit to help you in your prayers?
- If God knows everything, and knows everything we need, why does he want us to pray?
- How do you compare prayer to the communication you have in every other relationship you have with, you know, people?
- Sometimes the baby is never conceived, the girl gets away, we don't get the job, or the child dies of cancer. With what you know about God, how do you deal with that and keep praying anyway?
- What is something you want to know God's will about? Can you pray for that now? Pray it a few times, he will answer.

Chapter 8

God Is at Work, Even Now

"And we know that God causes everything to work together for the good of those who love God and are called according to his purpose for them. [29] For God knew his people in advance, and he chose them to become like his Son, so that his Son would be the firstborn among many brothers and sisters. [30] And having chosen them, he called them to come to him. And having called them, he gave them right standing with himself. And having given them right standing, he gave them his glory." (Romans 8:28-30)

Have you ever met a know-it-all? A person that thinks they know every detail about everything? What is it that makes that person so irritating? Is it that they are so smart? Probably not. Is it that they do not mind sharing their knowledge with others? No, you might even learn something from them. What makes Mr. or Ms. Know-It-All so irritating to me is that they *don't* know everything, they just act like it. Oh, they know plenty that they will be more than happy to tell you all about. However, when it comes down to it we know they are acting with pride, bravado, and too much arrogance. As the kids say, they think they are all that! *We* know they don't know everything, *they* know they don't know everything, yet they are quick to correct us and tell us their opinions, which of course they spew as facts. What makes it even worse is that they spew their opinions as facts even when they are *wrong*.

But then again, what if someone really *did* know everything? How would that change things? Well, that would probably depend on *how* they let you know all the stuff they know. Knowing everything and being obnoxious about it is still obnoxious. Imagine someone getting every *Jeopardy* question right and getting more and more smug as they answered, so that it built up to a happy dance after each question. And what if it grew to the point where that contestant was yelling "In your face" after every answer? How long could you watch before you were rooting *against* that person? Could you even watch the whole episode? Not me. I would be yelling that it was rigged and calling for a congressional investigation as well as wishing some Old Testament curse on that person; perhaps they should get frogs or locusts invading their home. Just saying.

On the other hand, knowing everything and being gracious with all that knowledge would make them the coolest person ever! Imagine that same scenario where the person intentionally did not answer so that the others could have a chance. Imagine this champion answering all the questions and then donating the money to a favorite charity?! I would be cheering *for* that person to win it all.

What if, as the Bible says, God is all knowing and all loving at the same time? Is it possible to imagine that someone can see into your future and promise you something good will come to you? Well, God can do that, but most of us don't believe it. Why? We have been scammed by Ouija boards, palm readers, Tarot card readers, pseudo psychics, weird preachers, negatively bent insurance salespeople, and the daily horoscope. We have all put some faith in them and come up short, leaving us skeptical. Just because they can't tell our future does not mean that *no one* can. In the same way, just because I cannot dunk a basketball does not mean that no one can. Just because I cannot hit a pleasant note in the middle of a song does not show that no one can. Just because I cannot cure cancer does not mean no one can. I think you get the point.

If God is, like Christ followers believe, all knowing, then he can easily say that your best days are ahead of you, even if you don't feel it. The most skeptical among us will say "he could be lying," but that would go against his nature as a loving, grace-filled, giving, adoptive Heavenly Father. Others might say "What if I mess it up? Don't I have choices I have to make?" Good point, but would God know that ahead of time?

Which leads me to a very confusing part of God: he is timeless, eternal. He always was and always will be. When we think of who created God, we have to try and bend our minds around the fact that God always was and always will be. My best explanation for this is that we live our life like it is a movie, a video, or a streamed video. As one scene unfolds we try to understand it; we wait, and wonder, what the next scene will be and how it will lead the story. However, God sees our life like a snapshot, an Instagram post, or a picture posted on Facebook. All of the details of our lives are shown in that one picture all at the same time.

Have you ever looked through a book called *Where's Waldo?* In those books Waldo is doing something in a very complicated sketch of dozens of other Waldo look-alikes doing their own tasks. Because so many things look like

Waldo it is hard to find him, but that is the trick, to find where Waldo is, and what he is undertaking. Now imagine that all those pictures actually were Waldo doing all thosee things. I think that is how an eternal God sees your life and can honestly say that your best days are ahead. He sees the part of the story we are in, the part of the story that is developing, the end of the story, and all of the good that comes in between.

One more mind-bender about God: he has already promised a happy ending to those who follow him. He has given us a glimpse of what our eternity will be like with him. In the last book of the Bible, the Apostle John has some visions from God that describe the ending like this: **"I heard a loud shout from the throne, saying, "Look, God's home is now among his people! He will live with them, and they will be his people. God himself will be with them. [4] He will wipe every tear from their eyes, and there will be no more death or sorrow or crying or pain. All these things are gone forever." [5] And the one sitting on the throne said, "Look, I am making everything new!"" (Revelation 21:3-5)**

It is easy for God to promise good in your future since he is the one writing the last chapter. **Is God working things together for good? He already has.** He provided Jesus to give us forgiveness for our sins, he has secured a place for us where there is no more suffering, he has given us the Holy Spirit as a helper and counselor, and he has adopted us into his family. All of that sounds like great news to me!

In the meantime, lots of us go through really painful and crappy circumstances. Many times, if you are like me, you wonder where God is in *those* situations. Heaven might be cool in the future, but where is God now? Paul says here that God **"causes everything to work together for the good of those who love God and are called according to his purpose" (Romans 8:28)** but not everything *feels* like it is for my good.

My sister died of heart disease, leaving a high-school-aged granddaughter that she was raising.

Where is the good in that?

My mother had a stroke, a heart attack, and cancer in the same year.

Where is the good in that?

Our friends' baby was born with leukemia and died at less than one year old.

Where is the good in that?

Another friend was following her son to work one day; he swerved, rolled his truck, and was killed instantly. As she drove up to the accident she had to see her baby's bloody, mangled, truck while he lay dead inside.

Where is the good in that?

I have known many foster kids in my life; they are batted from home to home through no fault of their own. These kids are there because of drug-using parents, abusive, or incarcerated parents.

Where is the good in that?

Too many of us know the pains of abuse, divorce, diseases, heartbreak, crime, substance abuse, gang violence, racism, and being bullied by someone.

Where is the good in that?

We, rightfully, ask where God is in all of *this.* In addition to that, we read that he is working for good and we can doubt, or just flat-out disagree and call Paul a liar. Let me be very clear: **God is working toward good in every situation; he is not *causing* every situation.** See the difference?

If God were causing all of that pain, we would have no moral, ethical, or spiritual business following him. If God were causing all of that pain around the world and around us, we would correctly see him as a cruel, calculating, twisted, bullying god that has no good in him at all. In fact, that would contradict the compassionate character of Jesus. It would go against when Jesus was filled with compassion, when Jesus wept over his friend's death, when he treated women and children with dignity and respect far greater than they were treated by any religious leaders or mainstream society. Indeed, Paul would have to completely re-write his letter to the Romans.

God is not causing the pain. God is, however, allowing people in pain to grow stronger, bolder, and help others in their own season of pain. I love how the Apostle Paul describes that process like this: **"God is our merciful Father and the source of all comfort. [4] He comforts us in all our troubles *so that* we can comfort others. When they are troubled, we will be able to give them the same comfort God has given us. [5] For the more we suffer for Christ, the more God will shower us with his comfort through Christ**"
(**2 Corinthians 1:3-5,** emphasis mine**)**.

God comforts us with his Holy Spirit, with his comforting words, and with other people. Then he works *that* together for good so that we can comfort other people who need it, just like we do. I cannot imagine my life without the comforting words of those who have suffered before me. I have been tremendously blessed in my life by those who have traveled down a miserable road and came out more compassionate than ever.

I remember when my youngest son, Caleb, was in the hospital and neck-deep into his litany of chemotherapies. He was in the middle of spending 161 nights in the hospital and had already had one trip to the intensive care unit. The doctors, nurses, family members, and Caleb had encouraged us to get away for the weekend to Camp Okizu, a camp for pediatric cancer survivors, patients, and their families. I remember how little hope I was feeling at that time about his treatments and his prognosis. I also remember how powerful another mom's words were when she told me she had been in the same seat I was in. She had seen her daughter suffer with leukemia, chemotherapy, and the ICU. She had worried about planning a funeral for her daughter. She had worried how the treatments would devastate her baby girl. She also told us that her daughter had gotten better and was going back to school the very next day.

Was the little girl's cancer good? No way.
Did God use that for good in my life? You bet! Hope was instantly restored and I grew a new vision for how I could encourage others as they go down that same pediatric cancer road. Has God used our story for good in other

people's lives? We have told our story hundreds of times and people have told me how encouraged they have been by our faithfulness, our story, and our compassion. God has also put it on my heart to raise money for leukemia research, and I have done that for the last eleven years. God has used that battle to give Caleb an incredible amount of positivity, grit, and determination.

Do we think God inflicted cancer into Caleb's blood?

No.

Do we think that our compassionate Heavenly Father was weeping alongside us as our baby boy suffered?

Unquestionably.

Did God use the cancer battle in our lives for good?

Undeniably.

Has God used our cancer story to encourage others?

We have been told many times: yes.

Because God knows the future and lives in a timeless space, I think he is working for good but we don't see it yet. Sometimes we only see what is in front of us, and cannot see how things will be used for good or turn out good. Yes, there are horrible, unspeakable, ungodly things that happen in this world. Neither I, God, nor the rest of us would find those things to be good. However, good can come *out* of all of those things.

Can I give you a few examples from the stories mentioned before?

My friends whose baby died might have lived if he had found a match on the bone marrow registry (Bethematch.org). In their loss and pain they began a crusade to get more people registered so that other families could have a chance at a match. They have been instrumental in thousands of people getting registered, and for a few matches along the way. God used it for good.

My friend whose son was killed in a car accident that had to witness the aftermath? She and her husband have grieved and still do. He uses his passion for cooking and barbecuing to raise money for a charity they named after their son (Ben's Closet) that brings medical supplies, food, and hope to a poor canyon in Tijuana, Mexico. She has led many others in the Grief Share program at her church, and now serves on the support team for their funeral services at church. God has worked some good in their lives. God has used their journey to help many, many others.

Your pain has taken a toll on you and your family, but God wants to use that for some good in your life. He wants to use it to help others, if you will let him. God knows how to work *all things* together for good for those of us that will let him do so and are called according to his purpose. **He is doing it right now, even if you don't see it.**

What I have learned about God so far:

1. He forgives me, he does not condemn me.
2. He leads me and helps me do the right things.
3. He gives us real life.
4. He adopts me into his family.
5. If I follow God, my best days are ahead of me.
6. He gives me hope, and I really need hope.
7. I can talk to him, he will talk to me, and I can get his holy help.
8. He is at work, even now.

Questions to ask yourself and maybe a trusted friend over coffee:

- Have you ever had bad things happen to you? How did you deal with it?
- Have you ever been mad at God for making people suffer? What did you do with that anger?
- Have you ever seen anything good come out of someone suffering or from their life circumstances?
- What are the hurting areas in your life that you want God to heal or use for good?
- Is there an area where you feel called to serve or to help out? Those usually come from some area where God has touched your life. Go do some good there.
- Can you look back over your life and see places where God may have been working but you did not notice at the time?
- Are there people you know that are currently going through hard times and need prayer? Pray for them daily and see what happens

Chapter 9

God *Is* for You

**"What shall we say about such wonderful things as
these? If God is for us, who can ever be against us?
[32] Since he did not spare even his own Son but gave him
up for us all, won't he also give us everything else?
[33] Who dares accuse us whom God has chosen for his
own? No one—for God himself has given us right
standing with himself. [34] Who then will condemn us? No
one—for Christ Jesus died for us and was raised to life
for us, and he is sitting in the place of honor at God's
right hand, pleading for us. [35] Can anything ever separate
us from Christ's love? Does it mean he no longer loves us
if we have trouble or calamity, or are persecuted, or
hungry, or destitute, or in danger, or threatened with
death? [36] (As the Scriptures say, "For your sake we are
killed every day; we are being slaughtered like sheep.")
[37] No, despite all these things, overwhelming victory is
ours through Christ, who loved us." (Romans 8:31-37)**

I don't know if you have noticed, but fear sells. This is

nothing new, but it seems to be rapidly escalating in popularity. In ancient times people lived in communities and walled cities that kept strangers out, and they thought it kept themselves safer. You see, “stranger danger” is no new concept. People have been teaching their families and children about this for centuries. Advertising agencies recognize this and know they can capitalize on it if they do it right. Consider this ad: "‘Perhaps a burglar or a fire has not invaded your home, but if they should, they would get all of your money and valuables,’ warned a 1913 newspaper ad, touting the benefits of using the Merchants & Farmers Bank in Spartanburg, S.C.”*

Oh, you read that right, it was 1913. Just prior to World War I, a bank was playing on people’s fears to let the bank keep your money safe for you. Isn’t that wonderful of them? They keep your money safe, they invest it to make themselves more money, and then you get the privilege of paying a charge to take it out of the ATM. Isn’t that just super?! For the price of that fee, no fire or burglar can get our money and we feel like our money is safer.

As I write this it is the Christmas season, a time for peace and good will toward humankind. Yet all over my radio and TV are advertisements for security cameras, home security systems, insurance in case your phone gets stolen, and identity theft protection. It must be the perfect gift for the “realist” in your family. “Overall, Americans spent about $20.64 billion on home security systems in 2011, the most recent figures available, according to the business research firm MarketsandMarkets. And the industry is expected to continue to grow to $34.46 billion by 2017.”* Yes, you read that right too; Americans will spend about **$35 billion** on home security, and that does not include businesses’ security systems, guns, gun safes, or watchdogs. Does that mean we feel more secure now? It may help, but I’ll bet most of us still struggle to feel safe, secure, and worry-free. It is hard to feel too secure when the news programs and pop-ups are so scary so often.

It also seems like there are other areas we are spending money with the same hope. In fact, “Some 15.4 million consumers were victims of identity theft or fraud last year, according to a new report from Javelin Strategy & Research.” ** In that same article, Kelli B. Grant says Americans will spend about $16 billion trying to repair identity theft and fraud. Wow. No wonder people feel afraid, anxious, and are paying for some hint of security. People want to feel secure, but it seems that bad things continue to happen to good people. The cost of our false sense of security keeps going up.

Although all that spending should make us feel safer, there is some evidence that it is doing just the opposite. Jim and Marilyn Folk report **"anxiety disorders affect 18.1 percent of adults in the United States (approximately 40 million adults between the ages of 18 to 54)"**—National Institute of Mental Health. Current estimates put this number much higher; ***approximately thirty percent***, more are people who don't seek help, are misdiagnosed, or don't know they have issues with anxiety. According to The *Economic Burden of Anxiety Disorders*, a study commissioned by the ADAA and based on data gathered by the association and published in the *Journal of Clinical Psychiatry*, **anxiety disorders cost the U.S. more than $42 billion a year,** almost one third of the $148 billion total spent on the mental health bill for the U.S."***

If my math is right, we spend $65 billion on home security systems, $16 billion on repair of damages done, and $42 billion on fear-related mental health treatments. That's $123,000,000,000 spent every year to make you feel safer and more secure. My real question at this time is: with all of that spending, do you feel safe, content, and secure?

Most people would say it is helping, but we are not there yet.

All of this shines a light on the fact that we all *want* to feel safe, secure, and protected. **We want to know and feel that someone has our back, or is looking out for us.** We watch our devices or read the news and feel threatened, so we spend money on security systems. When we find out that is not enough, we take some medications, go to yoga, and learn to meditate, or get treatment to help ease our minds. We know someone or something should keep us safe, yet we have little trust in our neighbors and almost no trust in the government to look out for us.

Doesn't there have to be *something* better?

The Apostle Paul knew a little something about worry and anxiety. He had been imprisoned a few times at a time when family or friends were responsible to bring prisoners food if the prisoners were going to eat. He was whipped, threatened, and shipwrecked. Paul had been an enemy of Christians, something he earned after killing so many of them. In the midst of all of that, he did not take anxiety medication, he did not buy a home security system; to be honest, he probably did not even have a home to secure. Paul did, however, feel secure in his relationship with God. He wrote **"If God is for us, who can ever be against us?" (Romans 8:31)** His rhetorical question reminds us that when God is with us, nothing can stop us.

Yet our minds have been trained to think about who, and what, can be against us. We know that there is an anxiety-inspiring list of what can be against us: teachers, homework, bullies, unemployment, identity fraud, home security, cancer, death, robbers, murderers, terrorists, immoral business people, spiders, snakes, food poisoning... need I go on? There are *so many things* that can be against us.

Yet, God is greater than them all.

If God is for us then nothing else compares. Our worries come with knowing "if" God is for us, and Paul writes it as a rhetorical question. He is telling us what he has said throughout this chapter, throughout the entire letter to the Roman church, and throughout his life: **God *is* for us.**

I think that Max Lucado, an author hero of mine, has summed this up better than anyone I have ever read or heard: "***God*** is for us. God ***is*** for us. God is ***for*** us! Your parents may have forgotten you, your teachers may have neglected you, your siblings may be ashamed of you; but within reach of your prayers is the maker of the oceans. God! God is for you. Not *may be*, not *has been*, not *was*...but God is! He is for you. Today. At this hour. At this minute. As you hear this, he is with you. God is for you!"****

With a nod to Max Lucado, please allow me to break it down the way I think Paul means it: ***God*** is for you. Who is for you? God. Yes, God. The Creator of the universe. The Almighty, the Everlasting, the King of Kings and Lord of Lords, the Most High, the ruler of heaven and earth, the one who put the sun, that you see outside during the day, and separated it from the stars that you see on a clear night is *for* you. The one who gives grace, peace, and free will to all of us is for you. The one in whose image we were created; God is for you! There may be other things that help you and make you feel secure, but none are greater that God, who is ultimately and surely for you. You can talk about having friends in high places, none are higher than your friend, adoptive parent, and your God who is now and always has been for you. He cares about you, gives forgiveness to you, sent his son down to earth as a grace-filled loving example of how to do life, and *that* God is for you. The God who parted the Red Sea, walked on water, fed thousands with a little bread and fish, healed a leper, raised the dead, died for your sins, and raised on Easter morning is for you.

It is unmistakably clear that God ***is*** for you. He is, he really is. He has proven it over and over again. He created nature and beauty for you to enjoy. He created other people for you to feel love and all the other feelings. Perhaps the greatest proof of all that he is for you is that "**God showed his great love for us by sending Christ to die for us while we were still sinners" (Romans 5:8).** He gave his one and only Son to leave the peace and joy of heaven to come to the exasperating, dirty, drama-filled, and dangerous places on earth. He was not curious; he created it. He was not on a wild adventure; he was on a quest to give us a way to reconcile with God. Why? Because God *is* for us. No doubt about it. He has done his part to prove it, and it is true whether or not we believe it. He *is* for us.

God is ***for*** you. God is not against you; he is for you. Some may incorrectly envision a God who is looking for you to mess up so he can bring bad into your life, but that God is nowhere to be found in the Bible. The God I read about is for you. He is in your corner, he is cheering you on, and he has his arm wrapped around you, and he's walking with you when times are tough. He cries with you, feels for you, and hopes the best for you. He is not against you, he is not indifferent to you, he is not ignoring you, and he is certainly not stacking things up against you. He is for you and always will be. He is like that guy who gets a tattoo of his favorite team, gets season tickets, buys all the shirts and hats, and paints his face for every home game. The score does not matter, and the standings are just something worth a glance; they do not change his fanatical nature. God is fanatical about you and wants you as a BFF (Best Friends Forever) relationship with you. In this case he really *does* mean forever!

God is for ***you.*** Sure, God created others, but he is for *you*. Yes, you. If you are reading this right now or having someone read it to you, then I mean God is for *you*. There are about 8 billion people on the planet right now, but only one that has your eyes, your DNA, your fingerprints, and God created those things in a loving way to make you special and unique. **If you are a parent you know that you love your kids generally, but each one specifically; so it is with God. He loves the world in general, but he is for *you* in particular.** He has given you an individualized story, he has given you gifts and talents, and he has called you by name. Francesca Battistelli has a song that I heard on the radio recently. It is called "He Knows My

Name"***** (2014). I think it sums up that God is for *you*, individually, specifically, uniquely, and personally:

> **I don't need my name in lights**
> **I'm famous in my Father's eyes**
> **Make no mistake**
> **He knows my name**
> **I'm not living for applause**
> **I'm already so adored**

The God I have already described adores you. If he has a refrigerator, your picture is on it. If there are picnic tables in heaven, he has carved a heart with your initials in it. If he gets tattoos, your name is in a place where he can see it. If there is poetry in heaven, he has written such beautiful lines about his unending love for you. If there are freeway overpasses, he has tagged them with your name. If there are rap battles in heaven, he is bragging about how awesome *you* are. All of that has already been proven, as the Apostle Paul says in **"But God showed his great love for us by sending Christ to die for us while we were still sinners" (Romans 5:8).** He sent Jesus for us all in general, but to show his love specifically for you. Yes, it's true: God is for *you*.

God is for you; but God is not a doormat or an abused puppy that keeps coming back for more and more abuse despite whatever has happened in the past. **He is for me, but make no mistake, he is not *for* everything I do.** I most likely let him down on a daily basis. I turn my back, I do my thing, and I violate a lot he stands for; we call that sin. God is not *for* my sin. He is not cheering on my lies, my judgment of others, my pride, or my bitterly hanging onto hurts from my past. Make no mistake, God does not stand behind all that we do; he stands behind his promises, his practices, and his loving nature. He is *for* me doing better, *for* my relationship with him, *for* me becoming a better man, *for* me being a better dad, son, employee, husband, and friend. God is *for* me having more grace, more peace, more patience, more self-control, and a spirit that looks more and more like Jesus.

What does that mean to us? We are loved by a God who is for us. He has actively, repeatedly, responsibly, and overwhelmingly shown his love is for us. When I remember that, I am so grateful that God, who has every right to be disappointed in me, is for me and always will be. He makes me want to be a better man. I think that should change our lives, don't you?

What would you do if you *knew* God was behind you? Would you talk more boldly to your boss? Would you stand up to a bully? Would you stand up for someone else who is being treated poorly because of their gender, sexual identity, economic standing, or physical attributes? Would you go boldly into a new ministry? Would you face the pain of forgiving someone? Would you finally learn to paint or sing? Would you do something you feel gifted in or have some hidden passion for?

No matter how you choose to honor God, he is *for* you.

Knowing someone is behind us should give us a good feeling. Knowing that the God of the universe is crazy about us and will stand with us for all eternity should give us all the security we will ever need. It should help manage our depression, decrease our anxiety, and remind us that the only security we may ever get is when we lean into the promises of God.

Make no mistake about it: God. Is. For. You!

What I have learned about God so far:

1. He forgives me, he does not condemn me.
2. He leads me and helps me do the right things.
3. He gives me real life.
4. He adopts me into his family.
5. If I follow God, my best days are ahead of me.
6. He gives me hope, and I really need hope.
7. I can talk to him, he will talk to me, and I can get his holy and powerful help.
8. He is at work, even now.
9. God *is* on my side, he *is* for me.

Questions to ask yourself and maybe a trusted friend over coffee:

- Have you ever felt like God was against you? How did that feel? Do you still feel like he was against you?
- Is there anyone on earth who loves you and is always your cheerleader? Who? What do they do for you?
- If you truly knew, down in your soul, that God was really for you, how would it change what you do? Or what you think? Or what kind of person you want to become?
- What are the areas where you want to feel more secure? Give those to God and see how it goes.

Endnotes:

*Jeff Williams (Contributor), "The Cost of Keeping Your Home Safe," www.usnews.com, Sept. 9, 2013 at 10:30 a.m. https://money.usnews.com/money/personal-finance/articles/2013/09/09/the-cost-of-keeping-your-home-safe

**Kelli B. Grant, "Identity theft, fraud cost consumers more than $16 billion," www.cnbc.com, Feb 1, 2017, 9:11 a.m. https://www.cnbc.com/2017/02/01/consumers-lost-more-than-16b-to-fraud-and-identity-theft-last-year.html

***Jim Folk and Marilyn Folk, BScN, in an article written for AnxietyCentre.com last updated April 25, 2017. http://www.anxietycentre.com/anxiety-statistics-information.shtml

****Max Lucado, *The Lucado Inspirational Reader* (Thomas Nelson, 2011), https://maxlucado.com/listen/god-is-for-you-4/

*****Francesca Battistelli, "He Knows My Name," track 3 on *If We're Honest*, Word Entertainment and Fervent Records, 2014, compact disc.

Chapter 10

There Is No Separation from God's Love

"No, despite all these things, overwhelming victory is ours through Christ, who loved us. [38] And I am convinced that nothing can ever separate us from God's love. Neither death nor life, neither angels nor demons, neither our fears for today nor our worries about tomorrow—not even the powers of hell can separate us from God's love. [39] No power in the sky above or in the earth below—indeed, nothing in all creation will ever be able to separate us from the love of God that is revealed in Christ Jesus our Lord." (Romans 8:37-39)

Susie and I once had every parent's panic moment: my son was gone in an unfamiliar place. I did not know where, and he did not answer when I called him!

My sister lives in Moss Beach, California. It is a beautiful Northern California beach community just south of San Francisco. It has world-class tide pools that often reveal starfish, crabs, tiny fish, lots of shells, some sea urchins, and various forms of plant life that I cannot name. There were many other treasures there as well, but mostly unidentifiable to me in terms other than "that icky stuff" or "you know those seaweed bulbs that we like to pop" or "that one thing that closes up when you toss a pebble into it." The tide pools sit among long sandy beaches as far as you can see to the left and to the right; beaches where the waves come in and out in the most rhythmically mesmerizing way

For those of you who don't have beaches near you, trust me on this: sitting and watching the waves come and go is an afternoon well spent. You can see why we loved taking our children there to explore nature, commune with the ocean, get their hands dirty, and be with creatures who would be unlikely to hurt them. Of course, I don't know what they are called, so how would I know if they could hurt us or not?!

One morning in particular, about eight o'clock, we were getting ready to walk down the one-mile-ish walk through a coast-side neighborhood to the tide pools. The tides were out and exploration awaited us! My son, Noah, was about five or six years old. He was a real Argonaut and a little hyperactive, so waiting for his parents to get ready to go to the sea was as painful as it gets for a young boy. He was ready long before we were. In our defense, all he had to get ready was himself, with our help. We, on the other hand, had to get drinks, snacks, stroller, and any number of other child-friendly gadgets we might possibly need. I am convinced that if Lewis and Clark had lived in our time and were taking a child with them on their trek they would have *never* completed their journey. They would have left late every day and all of that child-necessary gear piled up would have sunk their canoes!

My wife and I had gotten the kid gear, had gotten jackets and everything we needed for our adventure. We hurried out the door, locked it behind us, and hustled down the outside stairs to the ground floor and our awaiting escapade. It was a millisecond later that we noticed we could not see Noah anywhere. We peacefully went out to our car hoping that he thought we were driving to the tide pools, but still no sign of Noah. We began to call his name, but not a peep out of him. We agreed to surrender to a mini-panic and pick up our pace. We agreed to speed-canvas the neighborhood. I went to the left, Susie went right. We each were yelling his name. We each were doing our best Olympic race walking and asking complete strangers if they had seen our son. I am *sure* we looked like crazy people; we certainly were acting like wild, feral people. We both made it all the way around the block until we were back at my sister's house; still no Noah-sightings anywhere. Only now we had added the ten minutes of complete panic to our already morbid thoughts and review of every horrible thing the newscasters have said has happened to a child in the last year. It made for a putrid mix of fear, panic, desperation, and terror. His mother and I were a hot mess.

Through our tears, our fears, and our prayers we heard a most resounding baritone laugh. We stopped, we pivoted, and we felt a little crease in our dread. **For the first time in what seemed like a parental eternity, we hoped again.** I had forgotten that there was an apartment below my sister's house where she had renters whose revenue helped her pay her mortgage.

We went to the downstairs apartment door. We tried *not* to knock like we were a SWAT team, but I am sure it had some dread behind it. We were scared at the very molecular level of our beings that something unthinkable was happening. The door swung open. There stood a man. I mean, I think it was a man; at the time I thought he was part beast. He was about six-three and had long hair, the fullest beard I have ever seen, a tee shirt, denim pants, and an open forty-ounce beer on the card table that he used for his fine dining. Did I mention it was 8:00 a.m.? Not to judge what time to start drinking, but no bars were open. Just saying. To say he was rough around the edges would mean he had smooth areas, but I sure did not see them. He was rough through and through. He looked like he could scare the Hell's Angels, if he was not already a part of them. Man or beast, intimidating or puppy dog, we did not have time to decide. We were there to do a Noah extraction and not make friends. After some awkward conversation we were able to leave with our son in one piece, albeit hearts still racing beyond what our chests were meant to hold.

As we walked away with Noah, and when we were out of earshot of the man-beast, I was ticked off at Noah. In my most stern, fatherly, angry voice I said to him, "We told you not to talk to strangers!" Noah innocently said to us, "He is not a stranger, that's John." We left with our hearts in our hands, our fears relieved, and so thankful that Noah was safe and back with us again. Although safety tends to be an illusion, we were happy to think he was under our care again and that none of our worst fears came into reality.

Noah had been separated from us physically.
He had gone against our teaching.
He had been out of our sight, away from our desires, and out of our will. **However, at *no point* in this story was he outside of our love.** You see, our love for him did not change one iota. He was still our boy, still our son, and still had an enormously special place in our hearts. We spent the rest of the morning at the tide pools. We spent extra time hugging him, kissing him, holding his hand, and showing him all the great stuff that our beach adventure had for us. We loved on him as much as we could. Call it a reaction to our fears, call it a reminder of how much we love him, or call it whatever you want. Our love is real, deep, immoveable, and we wanted to show it.

Nothing could separate Noah from our love; not John, not being out of our sight, not being out of earshot, *nothing*. So, too, it is with God. Paul is so descriptive in his reminder to us that nothing can separate us from God's love. Nothing. Nothing? Nothing. It turns out that when you look into the original language of the Bible and translate its nuances and tenses, that word it still means "nothing."

Nothing you can name will separate you from God's love.
Nothing you can imagine will separate you from God's love.

Nothing you have ever done will separate you from God's love.

Nothing you have seen on the internet will separate you from God's love.

Nothing someone tells you will separate you from God's love.

Nothing you think about yourself will separate you from God's love.

Nothing you have been taught by your family, your friends, or society about yourself, your choices, or your behavior will separate you from God's love.

Nothing you have been told about your problems, your weaknesses, your mistakes, or irritating habits will separate you from God's love.

Paul goes on to say that none of these things can separate you from God's love either:
Can death? **No**.
Life? **Are you kidding me?!**
Angels? **Nah.**
Demons? **Not even!**
Fears for today? **Nope.**
Worries about tomorrow? **Nuh-uh.**
The powers of hell? **No, try again.**
And he goes on: "**No power in the sky above or in the earth below—indeed, nothing in all creation *will ever be able to* separate us from the love of God that is revealed in Christ Jesus our Lord" (Romans 8:39)**

I love that our feelings do not dictate the truth in this; God loves you whether you feel it or not. ***"But the great***

thing to remember is that, though our feelings come and go, his love for us does not." – CS Lewis. No emotional roller coaster rides here; just steady, smooth, unchanging, unending love.

Here is what is so great about this whole concept: no matter where you are with God, he is all in. He has already sent Jesus down as the ultimate sacrifice and ultimate sign of his love for you. You may be running from God, but he is everywhere and your fleeing from him will not separate you from his love. You may deny that he exists. You may be doing everything your way. You may be outright, actively sinning. You may be feeling nostalgic about how your relationship with God used to be. You may be feeling super close to God during this season of your life. **The reality is that *none* of that matters in the equation of how much God loves you.** His love for you is greater than anything you can, or will ever, do.

In other words, God loves you no matter what.
Nothing can make him love you more.
Nothing can make him love you less.

Nothing.

Furthermore, nothing can separate you from his love.
Nothing.
If that does *not* blow your mind, read it again! And again, and again until it sticks. It is life changing, or at least it should be.

It's not only an amazing fact, it is an even more amazing promise, guaranteed by Scripture writings and the wounds in Jesus' side, feet, and hands. It is a promise repeated here by Paul, but just like the words Moses told Joshua: **"The LORD himself goes before you and will be with you; he will never leave you nor forsake you. Do not be afraid; do not be discouraged" (Deuteronomy 31:8)**. This amazing promise alone should keep us from being afraid or discouraged.

Do you ever feel afraid, insecure, depressed, or discouraged? Come back to this promise and you can get through it. Things may not be working out for you in your job, your friendship, your hobbies, your car, or your money, but at least God loves you and will never turn his back on you. These are words that God himself reiterated to Joshua at his commissioning as leader of the people of Israel: **"No one will be able to stand against you all the days of your life. As I was with Moses, so I will be with you; I will never leave you nor forsake you" (Joshua 1:5)** From generation to generation of believer, these words and this promise has been passed on down. **Now it is our turn to take the words, juggle our fears, and embrace that God himself loves us and *nothing* will ever separate us from that love.**

If this is true for you (it is), how does it change how you feel about yourself? After all, you *are* a treasured child of the Most High God. What does this do to your fears? Oh, your fears may feel like they are hard-wired into you, but that is just because we all have rivers of fears and swarms of insecurities that we routinely have to navigate. **In spite of that, this truth remains: of *all* of the bad things that can possibly happen to us in this world, separation from God's love is *not* one of them.**

The God of the Universe loves you, and always will. He arranged the three-dimensional galaxies' stars to align in a way that, on a clear summer night, to make constellations. People have stared at those same constellations for millennia; we have named them Taurus the Bull, Canis Major, and Orion's Belt. That same God that set the moon in place, made it wax and wane to be full sometimes and a sliver at other times, loves you. The God who has made sunsets, rainbows, glaciers, roses, and babies that look so precious loves you. That same God loves that you delight in his creation. An old-time preacher, Jonathan Edwards, once said **"Nature is God's greatest evangelist."** I believe that all creation points us to a God who loves us and *always* will.

Long before our son Noah ever escaped our view on that panicky day, we loved reading to him. Every night, and often throughout the day, we would read to him. He would trustingly sit on my lap and listen intently to every word, every crazy voice, and imagine every scene. One of my favorite books to read to him was called *Guess How Much I Love You*. A baby rabbit stretched his arms up as high as he could to show his dad *how* much he loved him, but the dad's arms were longer. The bunny hopped, but his father could jump higher. The boy told his father he loved him to the moon; the father pondered for a minute and then told the bunny "I love you right up to the moon—and *back*." Your Heavenly Father loves you to the moon that he created—and back. In fact, he put the moon there as the measuring stick. In case that wasn't enough, he gave *his* Son to come down to us to teach us how to live, teach us what love is like, and remind us that nothing can separate us from his love.

Always remember that nothing can ever separate us from God's love.
Nothing.
Nada.
Zip.
Zilch.
Zero.
Nil.
Not happening, ever.

What I have learned about God so far:

1. He forgives me, he does not condemn me.
2. He leads me and helps me do the right things.
3. He gives us real life.
4. He adopts me into his family.
5. If I follow God, my best days are ahead of me.
6. He gives me hope, and I really need hope.
7. I can talk to him, he will talk to me, and I can get his holy help.
8. He is at work, even now.
9. God is on my side, he is for me…and you.
10. Nothing will ever separate me from God's love. Nothing!

Questions to ask yourself and maybe a trusted friend over coffee:

- Have you ever felt far from God? Why do you think that was?
- Have you ever cared about someone who moved away or died? How did that change your love for them?
- Paul says we will never be separated from God's love; then why do so many of us feel lonely? What can we do to change that?
- If nothing can separate you from God's love, what does that tell you about who God is? What good qualities do you think he has?
- How will you let this affect you? How will God's amazing love seep into your identity? Your schedule? Your thoughts?
- Now what? Knowing all of this about God's love, what will you to do honor God?

Chapter 11

Final Thoughts: Do You Get It Now?

Do you get it now? Do you see why I have such a love and passion for this singular chapter? Do you see why, of all the passages in the Bible, this speaks the most to my heart and soul? It is here that I find peace knowing that I am forgiven. Here is where I find my true identity as a Treasured Child of the Most High God. Here is where I can find comfort that no matter what I am going through, knowing that God himself is working to ensure that something good will come of it. Here is where I get the confidence that, as I walk through my journey, God has saved me from myself instead of condemning my poor life choices and poor spiritual choices. Here is where I come back to remember that I am not alone, God is with me and has sent me a perfect, God-honoring, heavenly helper who guides me and prays for me. Here is the spot where I am reminded, as often as I need it, that **God is *for* me**, never sending bad things my way, and never rooting against me. It is here, in Romans 8, that I am reminded that God gives me real life, real hope, real identity, and real purpose. It is here that I am assured that my best days are ahead of me. It is here that I turn again and again and again and again to be persuaded that ***nothing* can separate me from his love**. Nothing, no how.

If I had any super power, I know which one I would want. I would want the power to implant a thought into your brain, one that would never leave, and one that would be recalled many times throughout the day. A thought that would be immoveable, unchangeable, and impenetrable. I would plant in you the thought of how much God loves you, forgives you, is *for* you, and will never leave you. Okay, that might be a complicated thought, but I wish we could know that with absolute, immoveable, and unforgettable certainty.

Because if we did, we would be eternally thankful.

God has been so good to me that I am grateful and thankful more than I ever express. However, I am also thankful to the Apostle Paul for reminding me just how great God is! When I started to study the life of Jesus and the writings of the New Testament, forty years ago, I thought of it like binoculars. I thought that the closer I got to God, the more focused I would be. Things would become so much clearer until I finally got it all into focus in my life. I thought that once it was in focus it would be easy to live like Jesus, to be gracious, loving, and forgiving. **I have been wrong about that.** I realize now that for me the journey has been much more like I have turned the binoculars around. The more I know about God, the more it seems like I do not know much about God. The more I listen to theologians, the more I watch the Discovery Channel, the more I hear public opinions, and folks talking about God, the less I feel like I know him.

Like a compass that always points me to the direction of true north, Romans 8 points me in the direction of the one true God of heaven and earth. Paul has provided a target-rich environment to see God's nature, find a path for growth, relieve my fears, and remind me of my place in God's family and in God's promises. In short, I can look to this one chapter and see a condensed version of God's relationship with me. I can experience his truth and accept his promises to me. Everything about God seems to come into focus and seems much clearer to me when I am looking in Romans 8.

I know that not everyone will believe all of this, and thanks for exploring with me. Nevertheless, not everything needs to be believed in order to be true. I believe that my wife loves me. After all, she shows me, tells me, tells other people, and has written it a bazillion times in all types of greeting cards. All of those things help me believe that she loves me. Incidentally, if I did not believe she loves me, that would certainly change how I live, but it would not make her love any less true.

Here's an example: As I write this I am sitting at my kitchen table in my pajamas with some spare change in my pocket. Do you believe that? No, really, stop for a second and make a decision about whether you believe that or not. Imagine me, in my blue plaid pajamas, typing away on this book. I have pockets in them; where else would I carry my cell phone and my spare change? So, do you think I have change in those pockets at this moment? Now, here is my point. **Whether or not you believe it has no bearing on the pocket or the spare change.** In other words, if you do not believe I have spare coins in my pocket, it does not make the spare change mysteriously dissolve into nothing, or hop its way out of the pocket. It still exists. One more thing: the pocket change exists for all of us, not just those of us who believe that there is spare change in there. **There is no such thing as a magical quarter that is there if you believe it and gone if you don't.**

The same is true with God's love; his dedication to you, his desire to adopt you into his family, his leaving you a helper, being *for* you, and never giving up on his love for you. Whether or not you believe it does not change the eternal truth of all of it. **His love for us is real, and it is real for *all* of us; not just those of us who believe in him.** Based on your past, it may be hard for you to believe, but it does not make it any less true.

So, what about you? What do you think is true? Where do you fit into this story? I think you are wherever you want to be right now. It's a choice. If you want to sit on the sidelines and watch, then watch away, but that comes with a risk. You see, every gift receiver has a choice: open it, enjoy it, love it, or leave it wrapped, mysterious, and unexperienced. If you sit on the sidelines and wonder, you will do so with the unwrapped and unexperienced gifts promised in Romans 8.

However, if you want to follow Jesus then you are unwrapping a relationship that is bursting with love, acceptance, stability, consistency, hope, and help. All of that is what I have found as the foundation of my faith, and I found it in Romans 8. I have found that:

1. He forgives me, he does not condemn me.
2. He leads me and helps me do the right things.
3. He gives me real life.
4. He adopts me into his family.

5. If I follow God, my best days are ahead of me.
6. He gives me hope, and I really need hope.
7. I can talk to him, he will talk to me and I can get his holy help.
8. He is at work, even now.
9. God is on my side, he is for me...and you.
10. Nothing will ever separate me from God's love. Nothing!

I can tell you in all honesty that I have learned to love God in a more complete way. I have learned to trust God more. I have learned to look to him for help, comfort, hope, and my identity. I have learned that when I look to him daily, I am comforted daily; when I look less, I am comforted less. You do the math: I need more hope and help daily, so I look to him daily. If you are feeling less of those things, you might want to pick up your pace of relating to him.

What I *cannot* tell you is that I totally get it. I cannot tell you that I understand God fully or that I have it all figured out. I do not believe that I am the first person in the last 2,000+ years to get every belief and every nuance of God 100% correct. In fact, I agree with the nineteenth-century British scholar, who said **"A God who could be**

fully comprehended by man would be inferior to man himself, and less worthy of worship" - Henry Bompas.

As I said in the introduction, I am a simple man with a simple mind. If I could fully understand God, then that would mean he is, by definition, less complicated than I. On the contrary, I find God's ability to forgive me and not condemn me as confusing as anything I have ever come across. I find myself scratching my head in confusion when I think that there is nothing that will separate me from God's love, even when I seem to run away from time to time. His love is so big and far-reaching that there is nowhere I can go and nothing I can do that will overextend God's love for me. My nature is so different that I am dumbfounded by his grace, but eternally appreciative for it all the same. God's love, grace, and faithfulness are indeed the most absolute mystery in the universe.

I also mentioned in the introduction that I have been a psychotherapist for about twenty-five years. I have treated many people that suffer as they live with anxiety and depression. I know that there are biological factors that increase or enhance people's anxieties, traumas, sadness, and depression. Aside from those factors, I believe that there is so much in Romans 8 that can help people deal with their self-esteem. After all, we are loved and chosen through adoption to be sons and daughters of the Most High God. I believe that Romans 8 can help alleviate some guilt and depression. Moreover, God forgives us and we should forgive ourselves. Nothing we have ever done has changed God's love for us. God knows us better than anyone, and yet he is still altogether *for* us. I believe that the truths in Romans 8 can also help reduce anxieties. Furthermore, God has left us with a helper, has given us the relationship and the avenue of prayer to ask for whatever we need and to release all of our stresses. God has promised that our best days are ahead and that his glory is much more than our sufferings will ever be. God is a healer; Romans 8 reminds us that there is great healing and transformation in these words.

For those who want to continue this journey, continue to seek God's truth, and deepen your relationship with him, I want to give you a few challenges to help your journey:

A. **Read more of God's word**. It is full of hope, life skills, challenging lifestyle decisions, and imperfect people trying to live life the right way. I would say start with the Gospel of John; it is a compassionate, humane biography of the life of Jesus. If you want to live like Jesus, make sure you regularly look at the life of Jesus in one of the four Gospels (Matthew, Mark, Luke, or John).

B. **Find a church, small group, and a mentor who will help you in the journey**. Doing this journey alone can be confusing and maybe even risky. Hang around some people who are full of love and grace, who are trying to live like Jesus, and work with them in how to aim your life to do the same things. Not everyone will be a good fit for you, but find people who will care about you, be gracious with you when you mess up, and gracious with themselves whenever they mess up too.

C. **Worship God.** That is another way of saying express your gratitude to God for all he has done for you, given to you, and for his unwavering love for you. Here is an example:
[1] **Praise the LORD! Praise God in his sanctuary; praise him in his mighty heaven!**
[2] **Praise him for his mighty works; praise his unequaled greatness!** [3] **Praise him with a blast of the ram's horn; praise him with the lyre and harp!**
[4] **Praise him with the tambourine and dancing; praise him with strings and flutes!** [5] **Praise him with a clash of cymbals; praise him with loud clanging cymbals.** [6] **Let everything that breathes sing praises to the LORD!" (Psalm 150).** Go to places where they worship God for all he has done. Go to a place where their *style* of worship brings out the thankfulness and worship in you. Styles may vary; they probably all reach some people. Make sure

you go to a place that can allow you to stir your heart for God.

D. **Hold onto God's promises**. There are many in the Bible, and some will speak to you more than others. Someday I hope you have some favorites of your own. I have shined a light on many of them in Romans 8. Here are a few more of my favorites:

1. **If any of you lacks wisdom, you should ask God, who gives generously to all without finding fault, and it will be given to you (James 1:5).**
2. **"For I know the plans I have for you," declares the LORD, "plans to prosper you and not to harm you, plans to give you hope and a future" (Jeremiah 29:11).**
3. **Have I not commanded you? Be strong and courageous. Do not be afraid; do not be discouraged, for the LORD your God will be with you wherever you go" (Joshua 1:9).**
4. **Do not be anxious about anything, but in every situation by prayer and petition, with thanksgiving present your requests to God. And the peace of God, which transcends all understanding, will guard your hearts and your minds in Christ Jesus" (Philippians 4:6, 7).**
5. **"For God so loved the world that he gave his one and only Son, that whoever believes in him**

shall not perish but have eternal life" (John 3:16).

E. **Relate to God.** Serve him, pray to him, and listen to him. It is what a relationship is all about; it takes some work, but what you will get from him and learn about life is amazingly enriching.

F. **Reach out to others and teach them about God's love for them**. Others want and need to know about God's love for them. The Lord has gifted you with relationships that only you can reach. He has given you hope, given you grace, given you forgiveness. He is giving the same things to those you know and have yet to meet. Listen to what Paul says: **"Everyone who calls on the name of the LORD will be saved." [14] But how can they call on him to save them unless they believe in him? And how can they believe in him if they have never heard about him? And how can they hear about him unless someone tells them? [15] And how will anyone go and tell them without being sent?" (Romans 10:13-15).** He is sending you; don't be afraid to share this amazing message. Some people will reject him, not you. It is the driving reason I wrote this book, so that others will hear how much he loves them.

With my parting words I want to thank you for taking the time to explore this book, and I hope it will continue to inspire a journey for your life. I hope you find comfort within God's words, forgiveness within God's words, hope within God's words, and a loving relationship with a loving God through his words. I also hope you find people to go on this journey with you; I hope you find trusted Christ-followers who will be patient with you and guide you. I hope you find a church where you can worship God and interconnect with peers.

Lastly, I hope you can come to fully know and experience the merciful love of God who forgives you, sends a helper to you, adopts you into his family, opens a clear line of communication with you, promises a healthier and more hope-filled future for you, is totally rooting for you, and will never, ever stop loving you as you are, where you are, how you are, and who you are.

His love for you is simple, but enormous!

Post Script #1:

I hope you enjoyed the book. I wanted you to know that you are helping to spread this message of hope. **Ten percent of the proceeds of this book will go to sending young men and women to Young Life camps. They will have some awesome adventures and what promises to be the best week of their lives.** During that week they will get the chance to hear about the simplicity and enormity of God's love and that he wants the best for them.

Together we are making good things happen.

Post Script #2:

As your journey progresses, feel free to contact me with questions, comments, or stories about experiencing God's simple and enormous love for you:

stevemcnitt59@gmail.com
or, through Stevemcnitt.com

I would love to hear from you, interact with you, and pray for you. I am also available to come and speak at your church, youth group, leadership team, or conference.

About the Author

Steve McNitt has a Bachelor of Arts in History, a Master's degree in Social Work, and has been a Licensed Clinical Social Worker in California for over twenty years. He has been a Pastor, Speaker, Corporate Trainer, Psychotherapist, high school Social Studies Teacher, Coach, and Author. He has been following Jesus, studying, and teaching the Bible for over forty years. He loves to be part of unveiling God's truth with a splash of humor. He has had the privilege, throughout his career, to be able to make an impact in the lives of people in schools, churches, camps, businesses, mental health clinics, juvenile hall, and state prison (as staff, not resident). He is a father, a volunteer Young Life leader, and a volunteer for the Leukemia and Lymphoma Society's Team in Training. He has been married to Susie for over thirty years (in a row). He and Susie have two boys, both adopted, and both better looking than anything they could have produced biologically. He loves Jesus, his family, and a really good card trick. Throughout all of his life experiences, his greatest passion is for people to know the freedom and power they get when they embrace their genuine God-given, God-honoring, fully-loved-by-God identity. He has seen this happen again and again as people embrace the simplicity and enormity of God's love for them.

Acknowledgements

To my family: Susie, Noah, and Caleb, who have taught me grace, humility, and love. You guys tolerate my humor, my crazy plans, and my tabletop sermons. To my family, who taught me to take God seriously and, through our trials together, taught me unconditional love and resilience. I love you all! To Jamie McAdams, the first person to read this book; you gave me so much confidence, and energy to keep this moving. To Susan Salluce, who gave such words of encouragement and perseverance; this book is better because of you. To Amy Jackson, my patient editor and guide to all things editable (she may hate that word usage). To Nobie and Carol Hill, who mentored me and loved me before I knew I was lovable; by being who you are, you taught me more about Jesus than anyone else ever has. To Truls Neal—you have shown me grace, kept turning me back to Jesus, and have given me more laughs than anyone deserves in one lifetime. To all those Young Life leaders and kids over the years, you kept me focused on Jesus and not on religion. To my launch team who gave input on details I could not see by myself: Emily Adams, Sam Aguirre, Jamie Coffman, Ben Derienzo, Jen and Dan Heideman, Katie Kreps, Emma Lenz, Liza and Brian Martin, Brad Mitchell, Matt Molinari, Scott Rodgers, Sean and Erin Tangen, Bethany Wilkes, Brady Wilkes, and Olivia Wilson.

Made in the USA
Middletown, DE
21 September 2022

10408729R00099